THE APOSTLE ISLANDS— AMERICA'S WILDERNESS IN THE WATER

- PERFECT GUIDE FOR THOSE NEW TO THE APOSTLE ISLANDS

- CONTAINS LAT/LON COORDINATES FOR IMPORTANT SITES

- EXTENSIVE REFERENCE SECTION

- NAUTICAL CAUTIONS FOR BOATERS

- MAPS INDICATING IMPORTANT SITES ON THE ISLANDS

- LISTING OF OUTSTANDING PHOTO OPPORTUNITIES

- HANDY SIZE FOR BOATERS. KAYAKERS, CAMPERS AND HIKERS

". . .there has been, until now, a real lack of sailing information for boaters and kayakers who want to get up close and personal with the islands. . . It's a little like having a seasoned guide showing the best of what the Apostles have to offer." —Rick Olivo, *The Daily Press,* Ashland, Wisconsin

The Apostle Islands—America's Wilderness In The Water

ISBN 978-1-7347100-7-6

Library of Congress Number: 2008912051

Sixth Edition

Publisher: Silver Millennium Publications, Inc.

South Elgin, Illinois
www.silvermillpub.com

Cover photo: West shore of Devils Island

THE APOSTLE ISLANDS— AMERICA'S WILDERNESS IN THE WATER

A GUIDE FOR BOATERS, KAYAKERS AND BEACHCOMBERS

BY
LAWRENCE NEWMAN

Sixth Edition

CONTAINS LAT/LON COORDINATES
FOR IMPORTANT SITES

REVISED AND UPDATED

TO THE READER

In writing this book on the Apostle Islands, it was my goal to develop a concise and useful guide for those interested in exploring the islands. I've been coming to these ruggedly beautiful islands for more than fifty years and although I've traveled extensively, I return to them every year—to me the most beautiful and soul-satisfying place on earth.

I've been to all the islands, hiked most of their trails, walked many of their beaches, flown over, motored through, and sailed among them, marveling always at their beauty. This book is meant to serve as a handy guide to the boater, kayaker, hiker and beachcomber. Although there are other books that cover the National Lakeshore, most of those do not cover Madeline Island, the largest of the Apostles. I've also included lat/lon coordinates to assist the user in finding docks, beaches and scenic points. This information should be especially useful to those new to the islands. There is an extensive reference section to assist those wishing more detailed information on subjects associated with the islands. Most of the books listed can be found in bookstores and visitor centers in the Ashland/Washburn/Bayfield area and the Madeline Island Museum.

I hope you find this guide useful as you explore the beauty of these islands.

L. Newman   February 1, 2012

THE APOSTLE ISLANDS— AMERICA'S WILDERNESS IN THE WATER

A GUIDE FOR BOATERS, KAYAKERS AND BEACHCOMBERS

TABLE OF CONTENTS

HISTORY OF THE ISLANDS

The Apostle Islands, covering 720 square miles of western Lake Superior off Wisconsin's northern shore, were sculpted from 600 million year old sandstone by a series of glaciers that arrived around 2-½ million years ago and receded in the final period of glaciation about 10,000 years ago. Most of the beautiful stones found along the shores of the islands were carried by the glaciers hundreds of miles and dropped as they melted. It's hard to imagine the immense power of these rivers of ice, which were over a mile high. The weight of the glaciers caused the ice at its bottom to become pliable and flow south inexorably, gouging the earth as it went. The northeast shore of Lake Superior is still rebounding from the weight of the last glacier at the rate of almost two feet per century.

Initially, as the last glacier melted, the level of Lake Superior was hundreds of feet higher and only portions of two of the Apostle Islands were above water—Bear and Oak. Ancient beachlines can be found on both these islands. Later, about the time the pyramids were being built, the lake began dropping to its current level, uncovering the remaining islands. At some point Superior's waters began flowing towards the other Great Lakes in the vicinity of Sault Ste. Marie at Lake Superior's eastern end. One can only imagine the deluge of water that cascaded into the area, now known as the St. Mary's River, on its way to Lake Huron and Lake Michigan.

Over time, lake currents and the wind have changed beachlines, causing some islands to disappear and others to join together resulting in the island environment we have today—the Apostle Islands

1

archipelago. Humans have even had a hand in shaping the islands, causing Little Manitou, a small island off Manitou Island's southwest corner to disappear by blasting it with water and putting a navigation light on the pile of rocks that remained. The island shaping process continues today, as Long Island has become an appendage of the mainland and the "Hole in the Wall" sea arch at the northwest corner of Oak Island collapsed in 2010.

The early years of the 21st century have shown some substantial variation in Lake Superior's level, which is dependent, in great part, on precipitation throughout the year. The lake's level dropped almost 1-½ feet in 2007, a level not seen since the early 20th century. This drop caused some important changes in the islands' shorelines, dock usability and water flows into bog areas. However, the lake's level recovered to its earlier level in 2008, only to drop again in 2010—about ½ foot.

Although there is some disagreement as to how the islands got their name, the most widely circulated view on this subject is that the early missionaries coming to the area believed, or chose to believe, there were only twelve islands.

There are 22 Apostle Islands of which 21 are included in the Apostle Islands National Lakeshore. Only Madeline Island was not included due to the extensive residential and commercial development on the island when the national park was formed in 1970. In addition, a twelve-mile section of the mainland south of Sand Island was included in the park. Originally there were 20 islands in the park; Long Island was added in 1986.

The history of early human habitation has been difficult to document, although there is some evidence dating back five thousand years that humans inhabited the area, sometime after the glaciers receded. More recently, Native American oral histories indicate that the Ojibwe (Chippewa) migrated from the east to the Apostle Islands area about the time that Christopher Columbus sailed for the New World. Other Indian tribes were also active in the area including the Sioux, Huron, Fox and Ottawa.

Some 150 years later, around the time the Pilgrims were landing on Plymouth Rock, French explorers were making their way into the far reaches of Lake Superior, including the Apostle Islands. In 1659, two French trappers, Radisson and Grosilliers, established a camp at the southwest corner of Chequamegon Bay, located south of the Apostles and west of present day Ashland. During an active exploratory period French voyageurs established trade routes for their fur trading activities along the Great Lakes, including a portage route through the Brule River to connect with the Mississippi River. The French lost political control to the British in 1762 after the French and Indian War. Subsequently, the area became part of the United States after the War of 1812. The region was designated as part of the Michigan Territory in 1818, redesignated as part of the Wisconsin Territory in 1836, and eventually included in the state in 1848.

Following a comparatively quiet period, the islands and the surrounding area were involved in extensive development of their natural resources. This was aided by immigrants from Northern Europe, beginning in the mid-1800s, close on the heels of the opening of the Sault Ste. Marie locks at the eastern end of Lake Superior and the arrival of the railroad. In addition to the significant commercial fishing in the area, there was intensive lumbering in the islands and the surrounding mainland. In the winter of 1892-3 there were approximately 10,000 men employed in harvesting timber in the area. Most of the islands were harvested for their timber more than once. Lumber mills sprang up in the Bayfield area and along Chequamegon Bay. At the height of the lumbering activity, Ashland alone had eight sawmills running around the clock. The quarrying of high quality brownstone from the islands and the mainland provided building material for many of the large Midwestern cities. A prime example of this construction can be found in the building, formerly a courthouse, housing the Apostle Islands National Lakeshore Headquarters in Bayfield, which was built using brownstone quarried from Basswood Island.

The shipment of iron ore bound for Midwest steel mills from mines near Ashland was an enormous undertaking. Long trains carried ore to several docks in Ashland where it was loaded onto huge ore carriers, some almost two football fields in length. There were over twenty active mines supplying ore to the Ashland docks in 1892. The Du Pont Corporation built one of the largest TNT production facilities in the United States on Chequamegon Bay, providing significant quantities of the explosives for munitions used in both World Wars and for land clearance, mining and quarrying in the area. Ashland also was a major distribution point for Eastern coal. In May 1893 shipments of freight exceeded four million tons. Daily train arrivals and departures during that period averaged 385—both freight and passenger. Even with the bustling commercial activity in the region tourists came to the islands to escape the heat in the Midwestern cities and to view the area's raw beauty.

During the mid-1890s the Chequamegon Bay region was the second busiest shipping area in the western Great Lakes, surpassed only by Chicago. It shipped nearly twice the tonnage of Milwaukee, Duluth and Superior combined. One can get a feeling for the volume of shipping activity through the Apostle Islands during this commercial period based on one hour's count of 105 ships passing by the Devils Island lighthouse. If one could compare the horns, whistles, dynamite blasts, whining saws of the numerous lumber mills, the steam hammering in the quarries and the chugging of steam locomotives hauling their loads of iron ore of this period with the serenity experienced today, the contrast would be stark. The commercial boom of this period ended very quickly.

By the mid-20th century, the commercial fishing industry had collapsed due to overfishing and the depredation of the sea lamprey brought about by the construction of the Welland Canal around Niagara Falls. Brownstone quarrying ended much earlier due to new construction methods involving steel. Today's overgrown quarry sites contain brownstone blocks ready for shipping that lay were they were on the last working day. It's as if someone just blew a whistle and said, "It's all over, boys!" The quality of the iron ore taken from the Gogebic Range, east of Ashland, was no longer economically viable for iron production, resulting in the closing of the mines and the Ashland ore docks. Subsequently, the railroads that had carried the ore discontinued all service into the area. The large stands of lumber were gone and lumbering operations moved on to other areas to the north and west. The TNT plant drastically phased down operations after World War II and finally closed. Open pit mining in the West eliminated the need for Eastern coal distribution through Ashland. In a comparatively short number of years the area became what it is today. Only the tourists kept coming—and in greater numbers.

Time is a great healer and today the islands are once again heavily forested. In only fifty years, the time since most of the last lumbering took place, the white pine, the colossus of the northern forests, is beginning to show its future dominance as it breaks through the forest canopies throughout the islands. The cacophony of the earlier period of commercial activity has given way to the timeless sounds of waves lapping on sandy beaches and rocky shorelines, innumerable bird calls and the rustling of wind-driven leaves in the forest canopy. Today the islands are a veritable paradise for hikers, campers, kayakers and boaters of all types. The term "rewilding" has been given to the process of the forest regenerating itself and healing the wounds inflicted by man.

Since Lake Superior is the largest freshwater lake in the world based on area, its power is immense. It can create its own weather, and storms can be devastating. There have been many ships lost in the vicinity of the Apostle Islands, most prior to accurate weather forecasting. But even in comparatively recent times, large ships have gone down in Lake Superior's waters as evidenced by the fate of the ore carrier *Edmund Fitzgerald* in November 1975. The lighthouses sprinkled throughout the Apostle Islands were built in the late 1800s to assist the ships entering or passing by the islands. The islands also have been a place of refuge for the large lake ships transiting the length of Lake Superior. During most of the 20th century, it was not unusual for large ships to be seen at anchor in the safety of the islands waiting out lake storms.

The road that led to the islands becoming a National Lakeshore is an interesting one. The first attempt to have the islands declared a national treasure ended badly. In 1930, Congress ordered a report be made on a proposal for the Apostle Islands National Park. The inspector who was sent in accordance with Congress's request, Harlan Kelsey, a Boston landscape architect, was certainly not impressed with what he saw. The islands had just been stripped of their trees and had suffered extensive fire damage. It must have looked like a scene from a World War I battlefield rather than as a venue for a national park. Shortly after his trip, he issued a report throwing cold water on the proposal.

Some thirty years later, Senator John F. Kennedy made his first trip to the area on St. Patrick's Day, March 17, 1960, in his quest to win the Wisconsin Democratic primary for president. Later, as president, he returned on September 24, 1963. He flew into Duluth, Minnesota on the president's jetliner, *Air Force One*, and transferred to a helicopter. He flew over the islands and was impressed with what he saw. He always had a love of water and sailed extensively. He followed up his flight over the islands with a speech extolling the area's natural resources to 10,000 cheering residents of the area at the Ashland airport. Wisconsin Senator Gaylord Nelson, a Kennedy supporter, and an important advocate of having the Apostle Islands declared a national park, accompanied him during this trip. The designation of the area as a national park was moving forward when the tragedy of Kennedy's assassination occurred less than two months later.

Progress on the park designation moved slowly thereafter. In addition to the normal staffing changes caused by the presidential succession, the nation faced the turmoil and escalating costs of the Vietnam War. Budget constraints had an impact on the scope of the land purchases, size of the park as originally envisioned, and planned amenities, such as a scenic highway along the Bayfield peninsula. Senate hearings were held in 1967 and 1969, culminating in the passage of Public Law 91-424 by Congress in late 1970, providing for the establishment of the Apostle Islands National Lakeshore. President Nixon signed the bill into law on September 26, 1970. An interesting footnote to the Kennedy connection to the area is that his son, John F. Kennedy, Jr., came to Bayfield with a group of friends in August 1995 and did some kayaking among the islands.

Following the national lakeshore designation, the federal government went into action acquiring the properties from the islands' owners. Island properties under state ownership were transferred to the federal government. Private property owners were given three options: outright purchase; continued usage under a 25-year lease arrangement; or usage of the property until the last living person on the deed died, at which time the land usage rights would expire. Some of the 25-year leases were not finalized until the early 1980s so these agreements have only recently expired. Today, a few privately occupied parcels remain on Bear, Sand and Rocky Islands under the life-lease arrangements. See the York Island description page for the circumstances which resulted in a two acre portion of that island being excluded from the park.

In 2004, a wilderness area was established in the park, encompassing about 80% of the land in the Apostle

Islands National Lakeshore. This designation insures that the islands will not lose their wild and primitive character, but at the same time allows the public the access within the park they currently enjoy.

As a federal national park, the Apostle Islands National Lakeshore falls under the jurisdiction of the National Park Service, whose principal responsibility is to protect and preserve this national treasure. Funding by the government has been limited and recently a schedule of camping and docking fees was instituted to help the Service defray costs. In addition, non-profit groups, specifically Friends of the Apostle Islands National Lakeshore and the Apostle Islands Historic Preservation Conservancy, have been formed to promote an appreciation for, and preservation of, the cultural and natural heritage and the natural environment of the Apostle Islands. These organizations have raised funds to support park projects and events.

There are several important factors that have allowed the park to retain its wilderness appearance through the years. Most important is the intelligent administration of the National Park Service, supported by the community, which has followed wilderness principles, preventing any commercial exploitation of the islands. Another factor is the comparatively low number of visitors to the park, caused by the long winters. In addition, the lack of public transportation to the area and the absence of nearby interstate highways also result in fewer visitors. The park is simply not easy to get to. It's interesting to note that the projection of 920,000 seasonal visits set forth during the Congressional hearings on the park's establishment never materialized. The current level of annual visitation is approximately 200,000, and is not expected to rise significantly in future years. The reasons for this disparity in the numbers are several, including the fact that the planned scenic highway along the mainland shore portion of the park was never built. Critics of the park's establishment before the 1967 Senate Committee hearings pointed out that the type of fishing in the waters of the Apostle Islands (trolling) was not popular with sports fishermen; large boats were needed to boat safely among the islands; and the water was too cold for most recreational activities. These critics pointed out that more favorable areas for popular types of fishing, boating and other water-related activities existed on the mainland, south of the proposed park. These critics have been proven correct—to the benefit of today's current park visitors, since the waters, beaches and trails of the islands are uncrowded and provide the user with a wilderness experience.

In 2006, the Apostle Islands National Lakeshore was voted "the most pristine national park in the United States" by *National Geographic Traveler* magazine. The National Park Service, the citizens of the nearby communities and the returning visitors to the islands are united in their belief that future generations continue to experience the "pristine" beauty of these islands.

THINGS YOU SHOULD KNOW

Anchoring

Every year boats at anchor are driven ashore by wind and waves in the Apostle Islands. When anchoring in the islands the boater must be aware of correct anchoring practices and the current weather forecast, especially in relation to future changes in wind direction and strength. The weather can change quickly in the islands and a boat anchored in an area exposed to the open lake is especially vulnerable. Many times an anchorage that is adequate during the day during mild weather can be hazardous if continued into the night. A secondary anchorage should always be planned in case the wind changes.

Approaching Islands

Approaching an island's shore should be undertaken with a certain degree of caution. Review your NOAA nautical chart (#14973—Apostle Islands) and watch your boat's depth readings closely. Approach the shore slowly with a lookout posted on the bow looking for rocks ahead. When nearing islands steer clear of the areas directly out from corners and sandspits. Some of these areas can be shallow a significant distance out into the water. Obviously, the draft of one's boat is the deciding factor.

Beaching Shallow Draft Boats

It's normally best to come in on the leeward side of island. If coming in with light winds on the windward side, set an anchor at least 50 yards behind the boat's stern to assist in pulling it off the shore. If applicable, lift your propeller out of the water before beaching your boat and always tie a line from the bow to something sturdy on the shore. As a rule of thumb, rocks on the beach normally indicate rocks in the water.

Beachcombing

Walking barefoot on the cool sand at the water's edge, looking at the sculpted, sun-bleached driftwood and the endless variety of beach stones is one of the most rewarding experiences you can have when visiting the Apostle Islands. Many times the numerous shorebirds will scamper along the beach in front of you and occasionally you'll see footprints of the larger wild inhabitants of the island. Take all the photographs you want but leave what you find—with one exception. In the event you find obvious trash, such as cans, bottles, fish line, etc. please pick it up and take it back with you for disposal.

There are two special types of beach stones that you may find. One is white limestone containing fossils of coral or mollusks from ancient seas. The other is agate, which has been found on the beaches of Sand and Rocky Islands.

Bears and Other Animals

Bears are permanent residents of Stockton, Oak and Sand Islands and are visitors to some of the other islands. Not surprisingly, bears have been seen swimming between the islands. Recently, one particular bear, showing no fear of people, caused Basswood Island (2006), Hermit Island (2007) and Manitou (2008) to be closed to visitors. When hiking, make noise so you do not surprise a bear. The following cautionary words are included in publications of the National Park Service: "Never approach or feed a bear. Keep a distance of at least 50 yards, even for photography. Don't lure or allow bears to feel comfortable around campsites, docks and picnic areas. Store food and garbage in the bear-proof food lockers provided at campsites on the islands. Take steps to reduce food odors. If you encounter a bear in a visitor use area, make yourself look big, bang pots, yell, make noise until the bear leaves the area, and report the encounter to park staff as soon as possible."

Please understand that if you make a bear feel comfortable in the presence of people you may be signing the bear's death warrant since bears that frequent camping areas have to be destroyed. Obviously, being in close proximity to a mother bear with a cub is a situation to be avoided. If you see a lone cub leave the area quickly, but do not run. Chances are, the mother is close by.

Other animals, such as deer, beavers, otters and foxes are common on some of the islands. Coyote tracks have been seen on Oak Island. Although wolves are not common, there have been some recent sightings of them on Sand Island and crossing the ice during the winter. Since the range and the numbers of the gray wolf population in northern Minnesota and Wisconsin have been increasing, it's probable that the sightings of them will increase. Long Island, due to its attachment to the mainland, can harbor all the animals common in the area.

Birds
The Apostle Islands are a major migratory stopping point for birds preparing for or completing a trip across the broad expanse of Lake Superior. Large flights of birds are seen in the spring and fall. Many varieties of birds spend the summer in the islands. Over 200 species of birds have been identified either

migrating through or as seasonal inhabitants. In recent years, it has become a common sight to see eagles floating majestically over the islands, flying low along the shorelines or perched in a high tree.

Boating

Although the National Park Service (NPS) does not recommend the use of open boats less than 16 feet in length for travel among the islands, the current and forecasted weather should be the deciding factor. At times smaller boats are perfectly safe, and at other times boats of any size should stay off the water. The use of one's common sense is paramount to any hard and fast rules regarding boat length. The NPS also warns against overloading the rated capacity of the boat. The following excerpt is taken from a NPS brochure: "Boaters must obey U. S. Coast Guard inland navigation rules. Each boat must have: an appropriate personal flotation device (PFD) for each person on board, fire extinguisher, whistle or horn, marker lights, and a manual bailing device. All children under age 13 aboard boats underway must wear an appropriate PFD except when they are below decks or in an enclosed cabin." It is highly recommended that other boaters wear PFDs—as a minimum, the inflatable type.

In addition, depending on the boat's type and size, the following equipment should be carried: a compass, the latest edition of NOAA lake chart #14973, a cruising guide indicating nautical cautions in the islands, appropriate anchor(s), lines, marine band radio, cell phone, Geographic Position System (GPS) receiver, radar reflector, first aid kit, tools, spare parts and signal flares.

Other than Madeline Island, there are no facilities for refueling in the Apostle Islands, so plan accordingly. A common rule of thumb is a $1/3^{rd}$ of gas consumption going to your destination, a $1/3^{rd}$ coming back, and a $1/3^{rd}$ as a safety factor. Keep a constant eye on your fuel level. Fuel is less of a concern with sailboats that run on diesel but be sure you have a sufficient amount for your trip. Unless you're an expert sailor, you don't want to attempt to dock your boat in a marina under sail power alone.

It's also wise to have a float plan prepared before you leave and give it to a friend or leave it with a responsible person in the marina. It should indicate your route and expected time of return.

It is obviously the responsibility of a boat's captain to see that the consumption of alcohol is done in moderation. The penalties are harsh for boating in an inebriated condition, but more important is the potential loss of life which can occur. Dealing with rapidly changing severe weather conditions without the full use of unclouded mental faculties by the captain and his crew can literally mean the difference between life and death. With regard to illegal drugs there is a zero tolerance mandate on all boaters.

Camping in the National Lakeshore

There are **64** designated campsites on the national lakeshore islands. Other areas have been designated for backcountry camping. Permits with a required daily fee can be obtained from the National Park Service at the Apostle Islands National Lakeshore Headquarters in Bayfield. You should request the free brochure "Camping", issued by the service.

Both boaters and campers should observe quiet hours between 10:00 PM and 6:00 AM throughout the National Lakeshore.

Charts/Maps

The appropriate chart for boating within the Apostle Islands, NOAA Lake Chart #14973, can be purchased at local marinas, marine supply stores and the Apostle Islands National Lakeshore Headquarters in Bayfield. It can also be ordered directly from the NOAA. Special maps indicating hiking trails and other points of interest in the islands and on the mainland can also be obtained. See the "Charts/Maps" heading in the references section.

Docking Facilities

There are fourteen public docking areas on islands in the National Lakeshore. Few have sufficient depth for sailboats or other similar deep draft boats. The city dock at La Pointe on Madeline Island has sufficient depth but has no spaces for privately owned boats. However, the dock can be used to drop off and pick up passengers. Transient spaces are usually available at the Madeline Island Yacht Club. Some spaces at the public docks in the islands are reserved for excursion boats. Overnight docking at the public docks in the Apostle Islands National Lakeshore requires the purchase of a permit available at the islands' docks or from the National Park Service at their facility in Bayfield. Inquiries regarding the depths at the docks should be made before planning a stay at any of them.

Drinking Water From The Lake

The water of Lake Superior is the purest of all the Great Lakes, due in great part to the rock basin in which it lies. Few fish are found far out in the lake due to the scarcity of nutrients in the water. Crewmen on the large boats entering Lake Superior used to throw roped buckets overboard so they could enjoy a drink of its pure, cold water. Although definitely not recommended, due to possible contamination by *Giardia lamblia*, an organism that can cause intestinal problems, many people have drunk water directly from the lake. For this purpose it's best to draw water at least one mile off shore, not near any stream outflow, boat discharge or bird nesting area. Place your bottle/container at least six inches under the water's surface. To be on the safe side, water filtration devices available at camping outfitters, should be utilized. The water is safe for use in preparing coffee, tea and soup after it has been boiled for a couple of minutes.

Emergencies

Both the National Park Service and the U. S. Coast Guard monitor Channel 16. They can also be reached by phone assuming you have not exceeded the cell phone tower coverage in the Bayfield area.

National Park Service	715-779-3398
U. S. Coast Guard	715-779-3950
Bayfield County Sheriff	715-373-6120

Since the weather can change suddenly in the Apostles, it's always recommended that you bring extra provisions on any trip in the event you are unable to return to the mainland as scheduled.

Fishing

A Wisconsin fishing license with applicable trout and salmon stamps is required for fishermen 16 years or older. Deep water trolling is the normal method of fishing in the lake waters surrounding the islands. Inland fishing is prohibited on the islands—except Madeline. Be aware that there are fish refuge areas within the islands' waters where fishing is prohibited. See the Charts/Maps reference section for a chart available for purchase designating these fish refuge areas.

Among the more common trolling areas are along the southeast shore of Raspberry Island, the eastern shore of Michigan Island and between Madeline and Long Islands.

Flies, Mosquitoes, Ticks and Other Insects
In general, the worst time for flies is late spring and early summer. Conversely, the best time is late summer and early fall. Flies can be numerous on the beaches. Some varieties are simply a nuisance, others bite severely enough to draw blood. In general, the windless days are the worst. One of the best practices to avoid flies on a beach is to be on the windward side of an island. Some insect repellents have been found to be effective in warding off biting flies, e.g. Sawyer Broad Spectrum®.

"Hatches" of sand flies occur occasionally resulting in swarms that attach to the visitors in the immediate area. Although usually not of the biting variety, the attachment of hundreds of flies in a small area of one's body or clothes can be an unnerving experience.

The quantities of mosquitoes present are dependent on the amount of recent rainfall and local breeding conditions. They are usually prevalent in the island forests in large numbers—especially in the early evening. Use a repellent with a high DEET percentage to assure protection. As an additional level of protection, pretreating clothing with Permethrin® will provide a barrier that kills ticks and mosquitoes.

Two types of ticks are found in the Apostle Islands—the common wood tick and the less common deer tick, the smaller of the two, which transmits Lyme disease, babesiosis and ehrlichiosis. Ticks resemble flat, hard shell, dark mahogany colored spiders, and are, in fact, members of the Arachnid family. Shown below are the approximate sizes of the two types of ticks.

All hikers should examine themselves at the end of the day and remove all ticks they find, with tweezers just below its head, as close to the skin as possible, pulling slowly to dislodge them. Look carefully in body creases such as armpits and navel area. Although the larger wood tick does not normally transmit diseases it can cause an infection when it burrows its head under a person's skin. The smaller deer tick, as its name implies, must have access to deer during its development. The likelihood, therefore, of encountering the deer tick on islands with no deer is remote. A deer tick must be attached for at least 24 hours to transmit Lyme disease. If a person does get infected with Lyme disease, a rash, usually forms in the area of the bite. Flu-like symptoms, including aching joints, also are common. Similar flu-like symptoms are experienced for the other infections noted above. Anyone having these symptoms should see a physician.

There have been reports of swimmer's itch in the islands. Do not swim or wade near marshy areas and towel dry immediately after leaving the water.

Although a nuisance during the time they hatch, mayflies are harmless. They have a thin, wormlike body, about an inch long, with delicate large wings and are drawn to light sources in large numbers. Their hatchings are usually over within a week.

During periods of warm, dry weather in late summer grasshoppers can become plentiful throughout open areas on the islands and the mainland.

Another pest found in the islands that is harmless to humans is the Eastern Tent Caterpillar, which has periodic mid-June outbreaks in the islands. At these times, the infestations are heavy and can strip all the vegetation off deciduous trees, giving a gray-like hue to the landscape of the islands and the adjoining mainland. Healthy trees normally put out a second growth of leaves in a matter of a few weeks and survive. Park Service personnel have told of their experience walking down trails during the time of these heavy infestations and having to wave a stick in front of them to ward off the thousands of caterpillars hanging from the trees on silken threads. The Saddleback Prominent Caterpillar also has occasionally infested the islands stripping foliage from the deciduous trees.

There have been no reports of poisonous spiders (or snakes) on the islands.

There are two exotic insects that are threatening the island forests—specifically the Gypsy Moth and the Emerald Ash Borer. Basswood and Stockton Islands currently have the largest population of Gypsy Moths, which are devastating to oaks and aspens. The Emerald Ash Borer, as the name implies, attacks ash trees. While none of the borers have yet been reported in the islands they have been found in the upper peninsula of Michigan. In an attempt to control the spread of these pests, the National Park Service has instituted special rules regarding the transportation of firewood to the islands. Contact the Park Service if you wish to bring firewood to any of the islands.

Hiking Trails

There are about 50 miles of maintained trails on the islands, most of them on comparatively flat terrain. If you plan to hike soon after a rainy period expect to encounter patches of muddy trails—and mosquitoes. When hiking the trails in the islands, wear long pants and long sleeve shirts. Carry a container of DEET repellent with you and apply the repellent around your pants legs near your ankles and on any open skin areas, to protect yourself against mosquitoes and ticks. If hiking alone you should give your hiking plan to someone, with an expected return time.

Optional items, in addition to water and insect repellent, include food snacks, an extra pair of socks, foot powder, first aid kit, poncho, moleskin bandages, tweezers (for tick removal), a map with lat/lon designations, a cell phone, a camera, compass, a small pair of binoculars, a GPS receiver and an extended coverage two-way handheld radio connected to a camping or boating companion. You might even consider carrying pepper spray for use in the unlikely event of a bear attack. Obviously, the length of the hike and the total weight you wish to carry are considerations.

Hikers and other visitors to the park are encouraged to read the well-written foreword to the book "Hiker's Guide to the Apostle Islands National Lakeshore" written by Michael Joyner.

Kayaks

Since kayaks ride low in the water, boaters should always be alert for them, especially in wavy conditions. In most cases, they are easily seen since they are brightly colored. Kayakers usually travel in groups so if you see one, look for others in the vicinity.

If you are interested in kayaking contact the National Park Service at their Apostle Islands National Lakeshore Headquarters in Bayfield and request their free brochure "Paddling in the Apostles". See the reference section at the end of this book for a list of kayak suppliers and guides. The Apostle Islands Cruise Service will transport kayaks to or between islands for a fee.

Lake Superior

This huge lake, epitomized as the Gitchee-Gummee of Longfellow's poem *Song of Hiawatha*, is a powerful force on the environment of the Apostle Islands. Nestled in the southwest corner of the lake, the islands receive the full power of waves under west, northwest, north, northeast, and east winds—the worst being winds coming from the northeast, building power over 200 miles of open water. The lake is 360 miles long and 160 miles at its widest point. Its surface covers 31,700 square miles and contains 3 quadrillion gallons—1/10th of the earth's fresh water. The deepest point in the lake is found northeast of Marquette, Michigan—approximately 1300 feet. The depths in the area of the Apostle islands are much less and vary widely. The deepest areas are between Stockton and Michigan Islands and southeast of Outer Island. These areas average about 350 feet.

There are no tides in the lake although the winds can cause small changes in the lake's level on the windward and leeward shores—somewhat like water sloshing around in a pail. Seiches, caused by major changes in air pressure, can also influence the water level.

Occasionally, you will see a trail of yellow scum on the water between the islands. This is due to the pollen of trees on the islands and mainland. In recent years, green algae, caused by rising water temperatures, has been noted along the mainland coastline.

Lake Water Levels

The water level of Lake Superior can vary significantly between years. The early years of the 21st century have shown some substantial variation in Lake Superior's level. The lake's level dropped almost 1-½ feet in 2007. This drop caused some changes in the islands' shorelines, dock usability and water flows into bog areas. However, the lake's level recovered to its earlier level in 2008, only to drop again in 2010—about ½ foot. Consider these changes and adjust depths when using the lake charts. Inquiries of other boaters, marina personnel, cruise boat personnel and at sailboat charter offices should be made concerning current water levels in the islands.

Lighthouses

There are seven historic lighthouses located in the Apostle Islands National Lakeshore—the most in any national park. Most were built in the mid to late 1800's to assist ships in navigating through and around the islands. Lighthouses are located on Sand, Devils, Raspberry, Outer, Michigan(2) and Long Islands. Most of them are occupied by volunteers, who conduct tours June through August. During the summer, trips are made by the excursion boat from Bayfield to the Raspberry Island lighthouse. In early September of each year, there is a Lighthouse Celebration at which time the excursion service makes trips to other lighthouses in the park and provides the opportunity to participate in guided tours.

Navigation Warnings/Cautions

Move carefully around all sandspits and corners of islands, staying well off shore.

Avoid the area between Michigan and Gull Islands.

Avoid the area between Manitou Island and Little Manitou Light.

Sailboats and deep draft vessels should avoid the northern gap between Rocky and South Twin Islands.

Avoid the area between the southeast corner of Sand Island and the mainland.

Avoid the area between Grant's Point and the navigation buoy in the channel off Madeline Island.

Avoid the areas around Eagle and Gull Islands.

Be careful rounding Presque Isle Point on Stockton Island, staying at least 200 yards off shore.

Stay well offshore of the northern point of Rocky Island—at least 200 yards.

Stay well offshore of Amnicon Point of Madeline Island—at least 200 yards.

Personal Watercraft

Personal watercraft (jet skis) are not allowed within the waters of the Apostle Islands National Lakeshore.

Pets

All pets should be on leashes not more than six feet long. Contact your veterinarian regarding a dog vaccine for Lyme disease in the event your dog will be exposed to brush on the islands harboring deer. There also is a vaccine for *Leptospirosis*, which is present in the area.

Poison Ivy

Hikers and campers should become familiar with the appearance of poison ivy since it could be found anywhere in the islands, although the reports are rare—with one exception. Long Island has been notorious for having large patches of poison ivy. Best to follow the old adage "Leaves of three—let it be". See the website poison-ivy.com for good photos to aid in identification.

Ponds and Gill Nets

Boaters should keep a sharp eye for, and steer well clear of, pond nets identified by poles protruding from the water, net buoys and floating plastic bottles that mark the location of commercial fishing nets.

Recommended Experiences/Photo Opportunities

- View from bluff next to Big Bay Town Park picnic area on Madeline Island.
- View from bog overlook on Julian Bay Trail on Stockton Island.

- View of sea caves at north end of Devils Island from the water.
- View of sea caves at Swallow Point on Sand Island from the water.
- Walk along Julian Bay Beach and Tombolo Trail on Stockton Island.
- View of Mawike Bay (Squaw Bay) Caves on mainland from the water.
- Walk along the sandspit on Michigan Island.
- Walk along sandspit on Outer Island.
- View from the Oak Island overlook.
- View from Raspberry Island overlook.
- Hike to Sand Island Lighthouse from East Bay dock.
- View of high cliffs on north side of Oak Island from water.
- View of the stars above the Apostle Islands on a moonless night.
- View of Lighthouse Bay from trail ¼ mile south of Sand Island Lighthouse.
- View of Sand Island Lighthouse from the water.
- View of Sand Island Lighthouse from billion year old sandstone ledge.
- View of Raspberry Island Lighthouse from the water.
- View of the Aurora Borealis shimmering across the northern sky.
- Hike from East Beach sandspit on Raspberry Island to the lighthouse complex.
- Hike around Presque Isle Point on Stockton Island (Anderson Point Trail).
- Walk along Big Bay beach on Madeline Island.
- Taking the ferry to Madeline Island from Bayfield.
- View from sandstone cliffs of Big Bay Point on Madeline Island.

- View of a sunrise or sunset over the open expanse of Lake Superior.
- Visit to Apostle Islands National Lakeshore Headquarters in Bayfield.
- Visit to Northern Great Lakes Visitor Center west of Ashland.
- Visit to Madeline Island Museum.
- Visit to Bayfield Maritime Museum.
- Taking the Grand Tour cruise on the excursion boat out of Bayfield.
- Taking the excursion boat cruise to Stockton and Raspberry Islands.

Note: Upper deck seating is assigned on a "first come, first served" basis, so arrive at the loading area as soon as possible.

Scuba Diving

A permit is required for scuba diving within the park boundaries. It can be obtained from the National Park Service at the Apostle Islands National Lakeshore Headquarters in Bayfield. See Reference Section. Boaters should be familiar with the "Alpha" flag (blue and white) indicating divers are in the water and keep well clear of the area.

Sea Caves

A word of caution if you plan to enter into the sea caves on any of islands or mainland. Beware of large ships transiting the lake in the distance. The swells from their passage can arrive with tragic results.

Sun Exposure

Nothing will ruin a trip to the Apostles, or anywhere for that matter, faster than a bad case of sunburn. Exposure in an open boat on the lake and walking beaches over a period of hours without adequate protection will quickly lead to a bad case of sunburn. Unfortunately, because the cool breezes on the water tend to mask the initial stages of sunburn, by the time you begin to feel the pain, it's too late.

Wear a hat with a lanyard or a tightly fitting cap and apply sunscreen liberally to your face and other open skin areas. In many cases it's best to wear long pants, and closed shoes, especially if your skin has not been previously tanned. Apply protection to your lips also. Sunglasses are recommended.

Swimming

Due to the temperature of the water in the open lake, usually in the 50s during the summer, swimming is not recommended and can be dangerous due to hypothermia. However, swimming in the crystal clear water of the protected bays after a period of hot weather, can be refreshingly pleasant. Swimmers and waders are normally seen in Presque Isle Bay and Julian Bay on Stockton Island, in Raspberry Island's East Bay, and in Madeline Island's Big Bay. There are no lifeguards on duty in the park or on Madeline Island so all swimming is done at your own risk.

Trash Disposal

There are no trash disposal points in the islands— other than Madeline. Please take all trash with you for proper disposal on the mainland or Madeline Island. If camping in an area without access to toilet facilities follow proper sanitation practices, properly burying any human waste. Do not put any garbage or human waste in the lake.

Weather

Boaters traveling in the waters of the Apostles must always be aware of the weather forecast—and use their own power of observation. It's not unusual for a sky on a beautiful sunny day to suddenly turn ominous as towering cumulous clouds and the winds accompanying them announce a thunderstorm coming in from the west. Usually, sunny skies return in a matter of hours. However, it's always best to head for cover on the east side of an island at the first sign of a thunderstorm—and instruct everyone to don their PFDs.

Don't try to race a storm to the safety of a marina unless you're sure you're going to win. Get into the safety zone of an island or ride out the storm on the water. Nothing's worse than entering a marina as a storm hits. Chances are your boat is going to be damaged and you're going to cause damage to other boats.

Some storms can be particularly bad, generating large hail and winds strong enough to topple trees. There have been "microbursts" in northern Wisconsin with winds strong enough to snap off the top half of trees in a large area, radiating out from the point where the downward rush of wind hit the ground (Phillips, Wisconsin, July 4, 1977 and Brule, Wisconsin, July 3, 1983). There was even a tornado recorded west of Ashland in the 1920s. Fortunately, these occurrences are rare. The usual pattern of a typical summer day in the Apostle Islands is calm weather in the morning, winds picking up during the day, and a return to calm in the evening.

Typically summer winds vary between 6-12 miles per hour. However, in a storm, winds can be as high as 60 miles an hour, creating large waves up to 12 feet, especially in the waters of the outer islands. Marine forecasts should be monitored frequently when boating in the islands. Fog also can appear with little warning. Fog that is present in the early morning normally burns off by late morning as the sun rises. However, advection fog, common in the spring and early summer, can hang on all day. Prudent boaters will remain at the marina or at anchor until visibility improves.

Summer temperatures can vary widely. Although most summer days have temperatures in the 70's and nights in the lower 60's, the thermometer can approach 100° during an extreme heat wave. There also have been reports of rare snowflakes in July. Be prepared to peel off or add on layers of clothes. You can expect a 10-15 degree difference between the land temperature and the on-water temperature due to the cooling effect of the lake water. This difference will be more pronounced on warm days in May, June and early July.

One cannot overemphasize the influence of weather on a person's planned vacation. If the weather is good don't delay your plans—weather in northern Wisconsin is fickle. Rainy, bone-chilling northeasterly winds that blow for days under leaden skies are not an uncommon occurrence in northern Wisconsin. If your vacation or long weekend falls during the time of these northeasterly blows you've drawn the short straw in the weather lottery. One of the worst mistakes a boater can make is to force a planned activity in the face of bad weather. There are times you should stay off the water. Appreciate wonderful weather when you get it and resign yourself to bad weather situations when they occur.

A Helpful Acronym

As an aid to those who wish to remember the names of all the Apostle Islands here's an acronym that should be helpful—DR BOB SHORE'S MOMMY CLINGS.   (My apologies to any doctors named Bob Shore).

<u>D</u>evils
<u>R</u>aspberry

<u>B</u>asswood
<u>O</u>ak
<u>B</u>ear

<u>S</u>and
<u>H</u>ermit
<u>O</u>tter
<u>R</u>ocky
<u>E</u>agle
<u>S</u>tockton

<u>M</u>adeline
<u>O</u>uter
<u>M</u>anitou
<u>M</u>ichigan
<u>Y</u>ork

<u>C</u>at
<u>L</u>ong
<u>I</u>ronwood
<u>N</u>orth Twin
<u>G</u>ull
<u>S</u>outh Twin

ISLAND DESCRIPTIONS
AND
LAT/LON COORDINATES

PREFACE
(Please read carefully)

The descriptions of the islands set forth in the following pages have been kept concise as possible. The acreages and dimensions shown have been rounded. Refer to the books indicated in the reference section if more exact measurements are required. Major beach areas are indicated along with some minor ones. There are other innumerable small beaches throughout the islands.

Pay particular attention to the nautical cautions shown in the island descriptions. These cautions are based on the actual experience of the author, other boaters, and inquiries of Coast Guard personnel, cruise service captains and sailboat charterers. Due to the nature of the geography in the Apostle Islands (glacier dropped boulders throughout) there may be other dangerous areas not indicated. Watch your depth readings, taking into account your boat's draft and current water levels. Make frequent references to your chart.

Latitude/longitude coordinates given are normally 100-200 yards off shore. Coordinates for buoy locations and harbor entrances are much closer. Minutes are shown to the nearest tenth. Take the accuracy of your GPS receiver into account when using the coordinates given. Since the accuracy of GPS receivers can vary, and lake levels change from year to year, use of the coordinates given are at the user's own risk. It is strongly recommended that boaters check the latitude/longitude coordinates given to their chart (#14973—Apostle Islands) before proceeding to their destination, reviewing the route to be taken for potential hazards.

The anchorage references given are all subject to the discretion of the boater giving consideration to current and forecasted wind direction and strength. Anchorages exposed to the open lake can be especially hazardous and should not normally be used as a night anchorage. Each anchorage reference is followed by a wind direction(s) for which the anchorage should provide protection. However, since winds can change quickly the boater must always be alert to this possibility and have a secondary anchorage in mind.

For those who have not seen the term "sandspit" before, it pertains to a tapered beach leading out from an island and continuing as a shoal under the water.

Toilet facilities in the form of "outhouse" vault structures are adjacent to most camping sites on the islands. Review the camping brochure available at the park's visitor center to determine available toilet facilities at specific sites. Additional facilities near docks or lighthouses are indicated in the island descriptions that follow.

Following are the major anchorages used by boaters in the Apostle Islands:
> Stockton Island—Presque Isle Bay
> Raspberry Island—East Bay
> South Twin Island—west side
> Rocky Island—east side
> Sand Island—Justice Bay

BASSWOOD

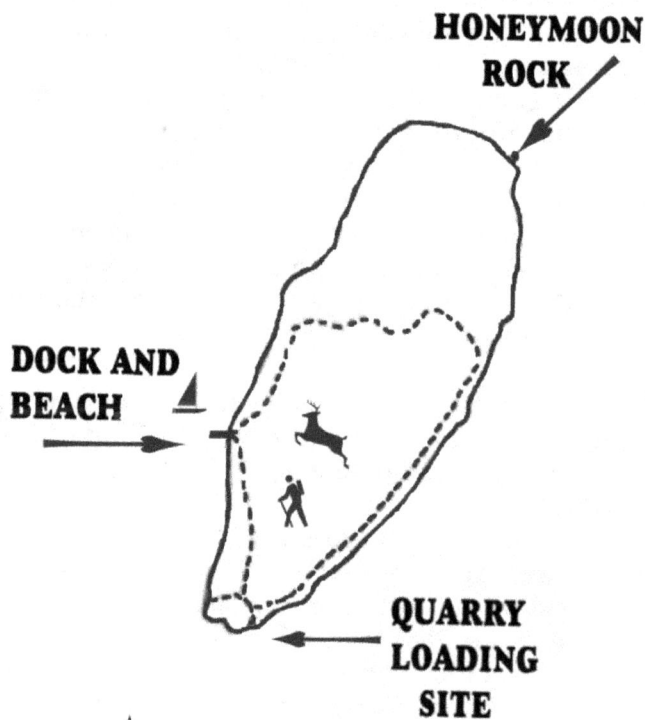

HONEYMOON ROCK

DOCK AND BEACH

QUARRY LOADING SITE

N

BASSWOOD
(1900 ACRES; 3 ½ MILES X 1 ¼ MILES)

Basswood Island is separated from the mainland by about a mile of water. It can be easily accessed from the Apostle Islands Marina in Bayfield and from the marinas north of Bayfield—Roy's Point Marina, Buffalo Bay Marina and Schooner Bay Marina. The island is heavily forested, but has a few overgrown clearings due to farms abandoned in the early 1900's. The island received its name due to the extensive growth of basswood trees that used to grow on it prior to the lumbering period.

Public Docks
A dock is located about a third of the way up from the island's southern end on the west side, facing the mainland.

Trail System
Basswood has a well-traveled trail to the south end of the island from the dock. An abandoned brownstone quarry is located there with a sandstone landing southwest of it. There is another quarry a short distance north of this one. The trail continues in a circle around the island. The trail leading north from the dock leads to the abandoned farms and connects with the trail coming around from the other side of the island.

Toilet Facilities
There is a vault toilet 200 yards south of the dock.

Water Availability

None

Points of Interest

In addition to the quarry loading site at the water's edge on the southeast edge of the island there is a large sandstone boulder named Honeymoon Rock at the northeast edge of the island. The brownstone used to construct the building housing the Apostle Islands National Lakeshore Headquarters in Bayfield was taken from Basswood Island.

Camping Sites

There are two individual and one group camping sites near the dock area and four individual camping sites at the southern end of the island.

Beaches

There is a small beach, about midway up the west side of the island, located in the dock area.

Nautical Cautions

Care should be exercised approaching the quarry loading site at the southeast end of the island from the water, as underwater boulders from an old crib are present.

Anchorages(Prevailing/Forecasted Winds)

North of the dock.
  (E, SE)

Lat/Lon Coordinates

Island Dock/Beach   N46°51.1'
                           W90°45.5'

Honeymoon Rock	**N46°52.4'**
	W90°43.5'
Quarry Loading Site	**N46°49.8'**
	W90°45.3'
Apostle Islands Marina	**N46°48.6'**
(on mainland)	**W90°48.5'**
Buffalo Bay Marina	**N46°51.2'**
(on mainland)	**W90°47.2'**
Roy's Point Marina	**N46°50.5'**
(on mainland)	**W90°47.0'**
Schooner Bay Marina	**N46°53.0'**
(on mainland)	**W90°46.2'**

BEAR

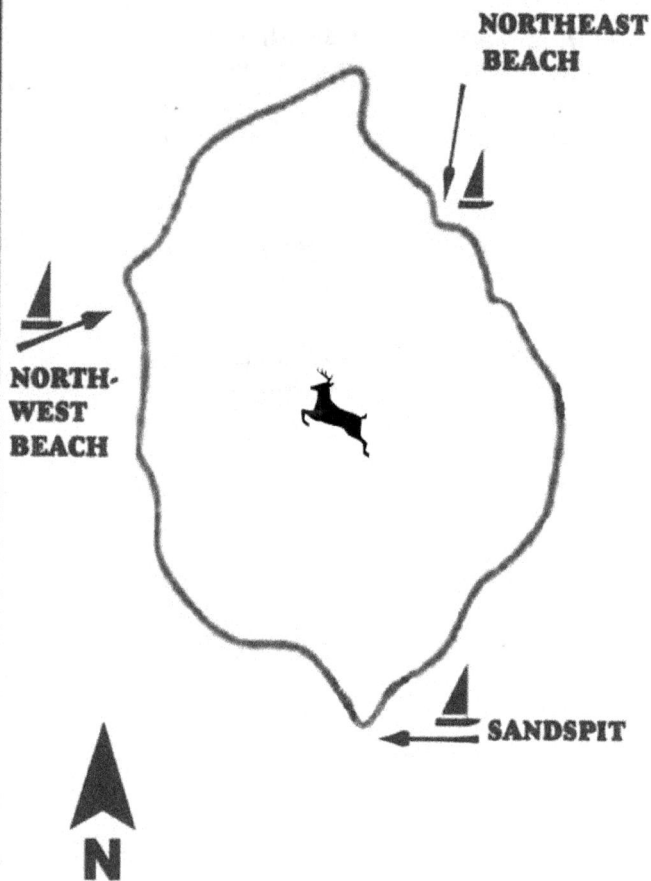

NORTHEAST
BEACH

NORTH-
WEST
BEACH

SANDSPIT

N

BEAR
(1800 ACRES; 2 ¼ MILES X 1 ¾ MILES)

Bear Island is the third highest of the islands and with Oak Island formed the original island group during the time when the lake level was much higher. An ancient seashore can be found high on the island. There is a sandspit on the island's southern point, with a nearby private dock. A portion of the island is held under a lifetime lease. The island is heavily forested and there are no maintained trails open to the public, making access to the island's interior difficult.

Due to this island's height it is one of the most recognizable landmarks in the Apostles. When viewing this island from the east or the west it has the appearance of a sleeping bear—the apparent basis for its name.

Public Docks
None

Trail System
No public trails

Toilet Facilities
None

Water Availability
None

Camping Sites
None

Beaches

In addition to the sandspit there is a beach in a small bay on the northeast side of the island and another on the northwest side.

Nautical Cautions

None

Anchorages(Prevailing/Forecasted Winds)

Northeast/northwest of the sandspit
  (W, NW, N)/(N, NE, E)
Open to the lake

In the small bay on the northeast side
  (SE, S, SW, W)
Open to the lake

Off the beach on the northwest side
  (N, NE, E, SE)
Open to the lake

Lat/Lon Coordinates

Beach-northeast corner   N47°01.7'
                             W90°44.9'

Sandspit-southeast tip   N47°00.0'
                             W90°44.8'

Beach-northwest corner   N47°01.2'
                             W90°46.6'

SAND ISLAND LIGHTHOUSE

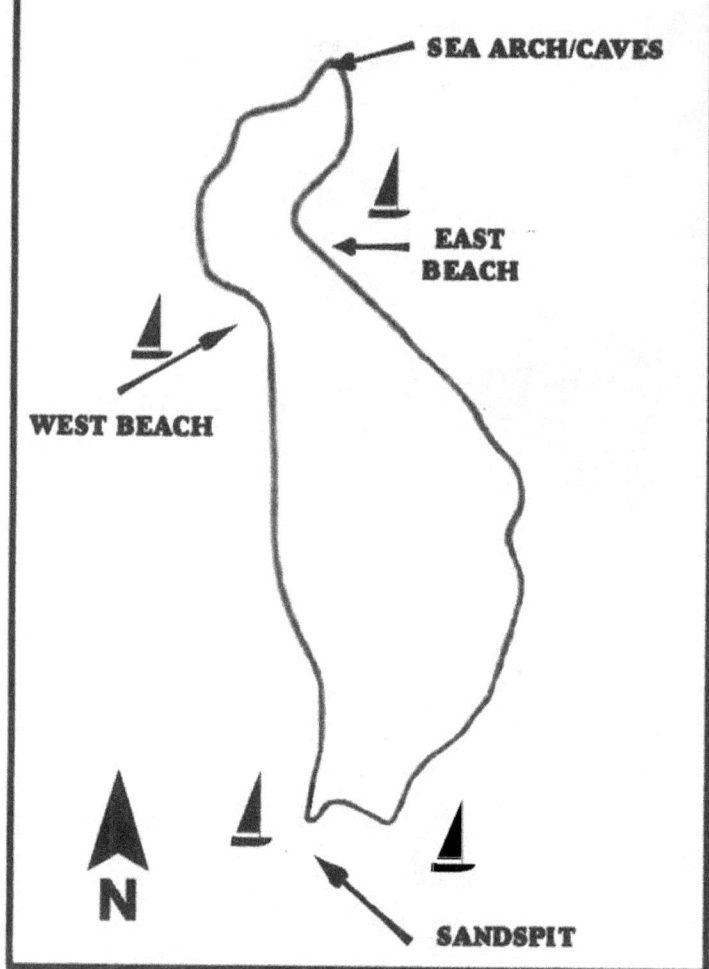

CAT

SEA ARCH/CAVES

EAST
BEACH

WEST BEACH

N

SANDSPIT

CAT
(1300 ACRES; 3 MILES X 1 MILE)

With the most optimistic view of this heavily forested island from above one could say it resembles a cat. It has a large southern "body" with a narrow "neck" at its northern end, terminating in a stunted "head".

Public Docks
None

Trail System
None

Toilet Facilities
There is a vault toilet near the campsite.

Water Availability
None

Points of Interest
There is a sea arch and sea caves, composed of a harder, less picturesque type of sandstone, at the northeast tip of the island.

Beaches
There is a sandspit at the island's southern tip and two long beaches—one on each side of the "cat's neck" on the west and east shores.

Campsites
There is one campsite on the west side of the sandspit at the south end of the island.

Nautical Cautions

Don't approach the northeast tip near the sea caves too closely as there are underwater ledges and rocks off the shore.

Anchorages(Prevailing/Forecasted Winds)

Off the west beach
  (N, NE, E, SE)
Open to the lake

Area east or north of the sandspit
  (N, NE, E,)
Open to the lake

Off the east beach
  (S, SW, W, NW)
Open to the lake

Lat/Lon Coordinates

Sandspit at southern end	N46°59.7' W90°33.8'
West beach	N47°01.5' W90°34.4'
East beach	N47°01.9' W90°33.8'
Sea Arch/Caves at northeast tip	N47°02.5' W90°33.6'

CAT ISLAND SEA ARCH

45

DEVILS

LIGHTHOUSE

SEA CAVES ALONG
ENTIRE NORTH
SHORE

ACCESS
POINT

DOCK

N

DEVILS
(300 ACRES; 1 ¼ MILES X ½ MILE)

This island, representing the northernmost point in Wisconsin, is one of the most remarkable of the Apostles. The wave-carved sea caves at the northern end are a photographer's dream, especially when they are bathed in the red hues of a setting sun. On a very calm day a small boat, kayak or dinghy can enter the caves.

Access to the island is limited in fair weather and impossible in strong winds. In addition to the dock at the south end there are two access points on the island—one located on the flat rock ledges east of the lighthouse and another on the northwest edge of the island. Both places originally had cleats affixed to the sandstone but these were removed in 2007. Rubber dinghies and other similar small craft can be landed on the flat rock ledges to the east of the lighthouse under calm conditions. If using the northwest access point, which is only possible in very calm water, fenders should be placed carefully to prevent damage to boat hulls and lines affixed to shore objects.

The island's name can be traced back to the time when the Indians inhabited the islands. The Indian name is translated as "evil spirit". Waves entering the sea caves during storms forced air up through blow holes in the island's surface, emitting strange sounds. It is believed these sounds were interpreted as those of an "evil spirit". The short trail from the access point on the northwest corner to the lighthouse passes by one of the blow holes.

A historic event took place in the summer of 1928 when President Calvin Coolidge and his accompanying party had lunch on the flat sandstone ledge at the water's edge, east of the lighthouse.

Lighthouse
Above the caves is a lighthouse with some supporting structures (see page 81). The Devils Light was not automated until July 1978, marking more than a century of lighthouse keepers tending the lights in the Apostles (1857-1978). This is the only lighthouse that still has the original Fresnel lens installed.

Public Docks
There is a small harbor and dock at the island's southern end that is shallow and rock-strewn.

Trail System
There is a well-marked trail, which was once a road, which leads from the lighthouse through a boreal forest to the island's dock and boathouse at the southern end. There are also two other trails leading from the lighthouse grounds—one to the flat rock landing to the east and the other to the access point on the island's northwest side. There are side paths leading off the trail to the northwest side of the island that allow photo opportunities of waves crashing against the west shore of the island. See cover photo.

Toilet Facilities
There is a vault toilet on the lighthouse grounds and another in the dock area at the south end of the island

Water Availability
None

Campsites

There is one campsite located on a bluff overlooking the dock at the south end of the island.

Beaches

None

Nautical Cautions

None, except for the harbor reference. See the cautionary note on page 27 before entering sea caves.

Anchorage

In front of the flat rock ledges, east of the lighthouse, 50-75 yards offshore, during the day, under calm conditions. Lake bottom is rocky here. Don't leave boat unattended. Take dinghy to flat rock ledges.

Lat/Lon Coordinates

Lighthouse/sea caves   N47°04.9'
                                     W90°43.7'

Access point east of lighthouse   N47°04.8'
                                     W90°43.5'

Access point on northwest corner N47°04.7'
                                     W90°44.0'

Boathouse and dock at south end N47°03.7'
                                     W90°43.6'

EAGLE

X ← POINT
NORTH OF
* ISLAND
N46°56.9'
W91°02.1'

N

50

EAGLE
(28 ACRES; ½ MILE X ¼ MILE)

The second smallest island in the Apostles after Gull Island, Eagle Island is at the westernmost limit of the Apostles. Access to the island is prohibited from May 15th to September 1st due to the island's designation as a bird sanctuary for gulls, double crested cormorants and blue herons. Although it is possible that eagles were seen on the island at one time, given its name, there are none on the island today. Approach to the island should be no closer than 500 feet during the restricted period. Although there are no beaches or trails on the island, it is not far from a beautiful beach on Siskiwit Bay near the town of Cornucopia on the mainland.

Directly south of the island, on the mainland, are the scenic sea caves of Squaw Bay (Mawike Bay). See cautionary note about entering sea caves on page 27.

Public Docks
None

Trail System
None

Toilet Facilities
None

Water Availability
None

Campsites
None

Beaches
None

Nautical Cautions
This heavily forested island is surrounded by underwater boulders, especially on its southern side, and is dangerous to approach at any time. Some of these boulders lie just under the water's surface.

Landing on the island's high banked shore should only be attempted by small, shallow draft boats or dinghies, under oar power, in calm conditions, approaching from the west.

Anchorages
None

Lat/Lon Coordinates

Point north of island	N46°56.9' W91°02.1'
Mawike (Squaw) Bay Caves (on mainland)	N46°54.5' W91°01.5'
Siskiwit Bay Beach (on mainland)	N46°52.0' W91°06.8'
Siskiwit Bay/Town of Bell Marianas (on mainland)	N46°51.8' W91°06.2'

RASPBERRY ISLAND LIGHTHOUSE

GULL

X ← POINT NORTH
OF ISLAND
N46°54.6'
W 90°26.5'

LIGHT
TOWER

N

54

GULL
(3 ACRES; 40 YARDS X 250 YARDS)

Smallest of the Apostles, Gull Island lies directly northeast of Michigan Island, separated by a boulder-strewn area. It is a bird sanctuary for herring gulls and double crested cormorants. Access to this island is prohibited from May 15th to September 1st. Maintain a 500-foot distance from the island during this period. Viewing the island from the east or west it looks like a one-masted boat, due to the navigation light tower on the north end of the island. The hard surface of this island is strewn with signs of gull activity—not a very pleasant place to visit. Viewed from the air the island is completely white due to the gull guano.

Public Docks
None

Trail System
None

Toilet Facilities
None

Water Availability
None

Campsites
None

Beaches
None

Nautical Cautions

Avoid the area between Gull and Michigan Islands. Access to this island of sparse vegetation is difficult due to the boulders surrounding the island as much as 100 yards distant from the shore, some exposed and others just below the water's surface.   Landing on the island's shore should only be attempted by small, shallow draft boats or dinghies, under oar power, in calm conditions, approaching from the southeast.

Anchorages

None

Lat/Lon Coordinates

Point north of island   N46°54.6'
                                                          W90°26.5'

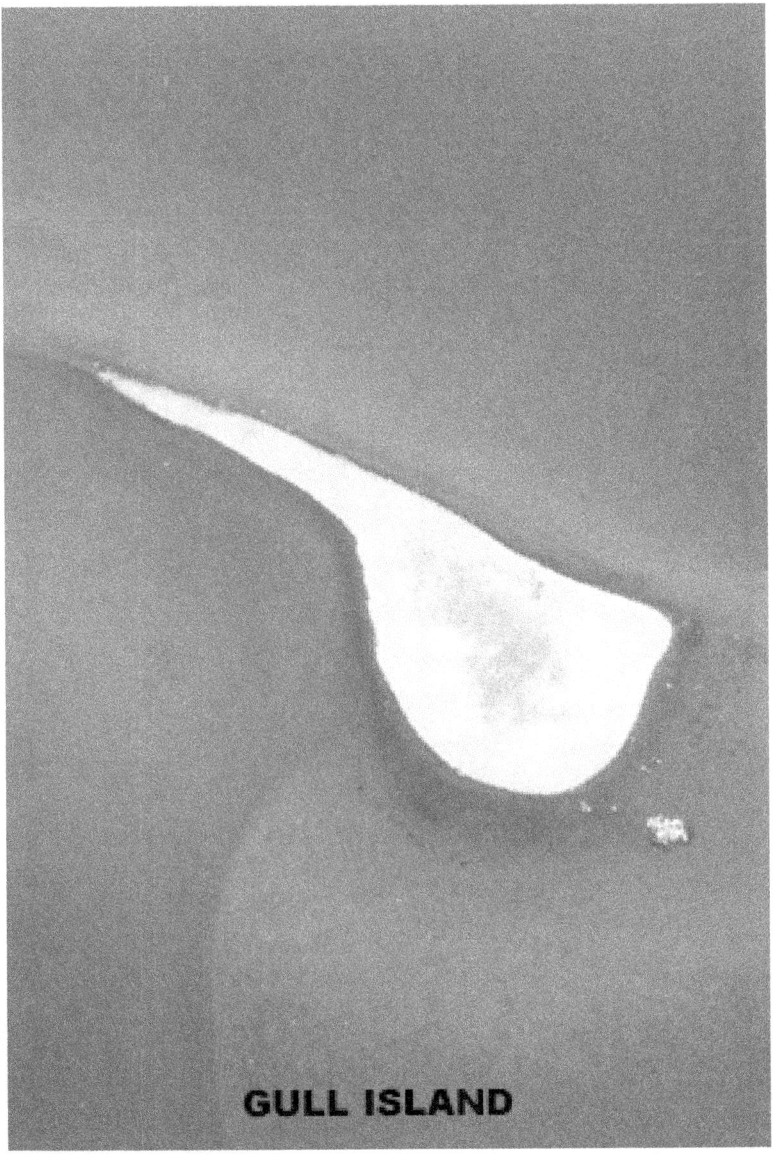
GULL ISLAND

HERMIT

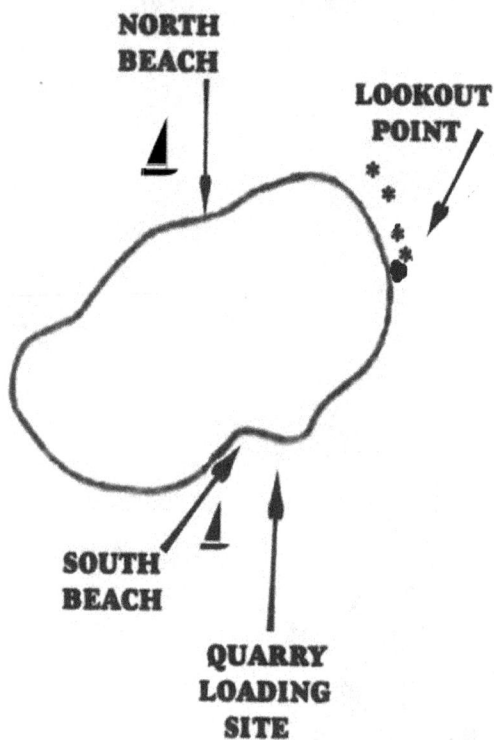

NORTH
BEACH

LOOKOUT
POINT

SOUTH
BEACH

QUARRY
LOADING
SITE

N

HERMIT
(800 ACRES; 2 MILES X ¾ MILE)

Hermit Island is located approximately midway between Basswood and Stockton Islands, on the northern edge of the North Channel leading from Bayfield to the lake. The island is heavily forested in most areas. Small waterfalls can sometimes be seen on the south side of the island, after a period of rain.

The island's name refers to an actual hermit who inhabited the island in the mid-1800s. During that time, and into the early 1900s, the island was named Wilson's Island, after the hermit.

Public Docks
None

Trail System
None

Toilet Facilities
None

Water Availability
None

Points of Interest
A sandstone quarry can be found about the middle of the island on the south shore. Lookout Point, a rocky column, in the shape of a boot, marks the northeast end of the island. At one time there was an arch here but it collapsed in the summer of 1975.

Campsites
None

Beaches
There are beaches on the north and south shores.

Nautical Cautions
Depths drop off sharply all around the island but boulders and rocks are just under the water's surface near the cliffs on the northeast end.

Anchorages(Prevailing/Forecasted Winds)
Off beach on the north side of island
  (E, SE, S)
Open to the lake

Off beach on the south side of island
  (N, NE, E)

Lat/Lon Coordinates
Lookout Point   N46°53.5'
                                       W90°40.0'

Quarry Loading Site   N46°52.8'
                                       W90°40.6'

South beach   N46°52.7'
                                       W90°41.3'

North beach   N46°53.6'
                                       W90°41.5'

HERMIT ISLAND--LOOKOUT POINT

IRONWOOD

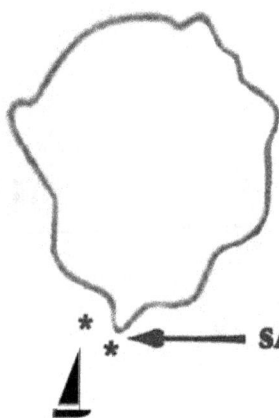

SANDSPIT

N

IRONWOOD
(700 ACRES; 1 ¼ MILES X 1 MILE)

This is a heavily forested island whose name comes from the ironwood trees that once grew profusely on the island before it was harvested for its lumber.

Public Docks
None

Trail System
None

Water Availability
None

Campsites/Toilet Facilities
There is one campsite near sandspit. No vault toilet.

Beaches
There is a sandspit at the island's southern end.

Nautical Cautions
Beware of boulders approaching the sandspit.

Anchorages(Prevailing/Forecasted Winds)
Off sandspit (NW, N, NE) ***Open to the lake***

Lat/Lon Coordinates
Sandspit at south end   N46°59.3'/W90°37.0'

LONG

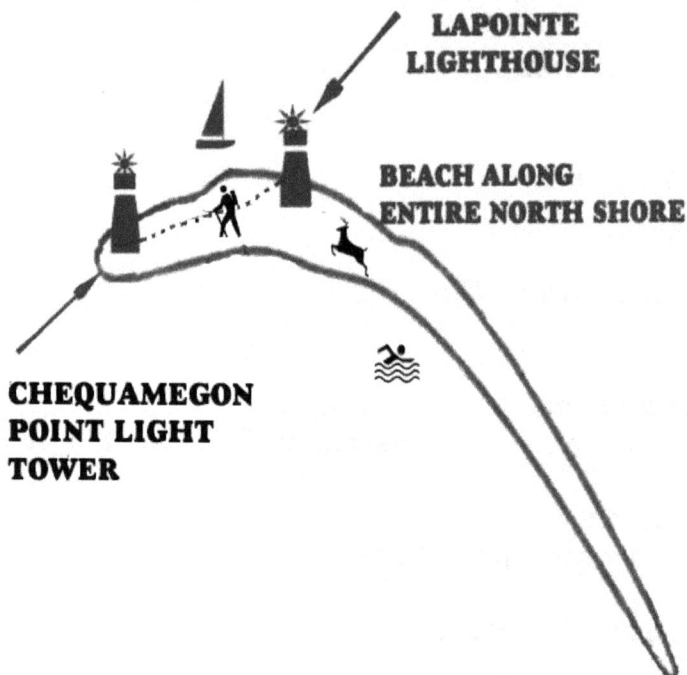

LAPOINTE LIGHTHOUSE

BEACH ALONG ENTIRE NORTH SHORE

CHEQUAMEGON POINT LIGHT TOWER

N

LONG
(300 ACRES; 3 ½ MILES X ¼ MILE)

Long Island was a late addition to the National Lakeshore in 1986, the park being originally formed with 20 islands in 1970. The island is composed entirely of sand and is considered a barrier spit. It is not actually an island and hasn't been for many years. Long Island is now part of an unbroken peninsula from the mainland. (See photo on page 85) The mainland portion of the peninsula, formerly Chequamegon Point, is an extension of the Bad River Indian Reservation. The last time that water flowed through the gap between Long Island and Chequamegon Point was the summer of 1976 following the severe storm of November 1975, that sank the ore carrier *Edmund Fitzgerald,* north of Whitefish Bay, at the east end of Lake Superior. Since that time the lake currents have closed the gap between the island and the mainland. It was a common sight in the first half of the 20th century to see sports fishermen move their boats through the shallow gap between Long Island and Chequamegon Point, using this "shortcut" between the lake and Chequamegon Bay. The basis for its name is self-explanatory and has been in use since the nineteenth century.

An historic event took place on the island in the late 1700s or early 1800s (the exact date is uncertain) when a war party of about 150 Sioux Indians was trapped and annihilated by local Ojibwe Indians. It is said that bones of the dead were still found on the island in 1850.

Care should be taken when walking along the beach on the island's lakeside as it represents one of the few nesting spots for the piping plover, an endangered shore bird. In addition to its blueberries this island also is known for having substantial patches of poison ivy so be aware of its characteristics and keep a sharp eye. Deer, bears and foxes have been sighted on Long Island.

Lighthouses

The island has a lighthouse (La Pointe) with a nearby two story lightkeeper's house midway on its north side and a large navigation light tower at its western end, marking the entrance to Chequamegon Bay, where the cities of Ashland and Washburn are located. The light tower stands next to an abandoned light station, recently renovated, that was built in 1896. No tours of the La Pointe lighthouse are conducted by National Park Service personnel. The fate of the Fresnel lens originally installed in the La Pointe lighthouse is unknown.

Public Docks

There is an unusable dock missing several feet near the beach in the vicinity of the La Pointe lighthouse (2009).

Trail System

There is a trail from the La Pointe Lighthouse to the island's western tip.

Toilet Facilities

None

Water Availability

None

Campsites
None

Beaches
A long deep beach on the north side of the Island is connected to the beach on the mainland peninsula extending all the way to the mouth of Bad River, a total distance of about ten miles. The Chequamegon Bay side of the island also has substantial beach areas.

Nautical Cautions
The Chequamegon Bay side of the island has very shallow water extending out from the shore for a significant distance. Check your chart. Depths should be watched carefully when coming around the west point of the Island into Chequamegon Bay from the lake side. Stay well off shore.

Anchorages(Prevailing/Forecasted Winds)
Anywhere off the beach on lake side
  (SE, S, SW, W)
Open to the lake

Lat/Lon Coordinates
La Pointe Lighthouse	N46°43.9' W90°47.0'
Western end of island (Navigation light tower)	N46°43.7' W90°48.8'
Eastern limit of Long Island	N46°42.1' W90°44.9'

MADELINE

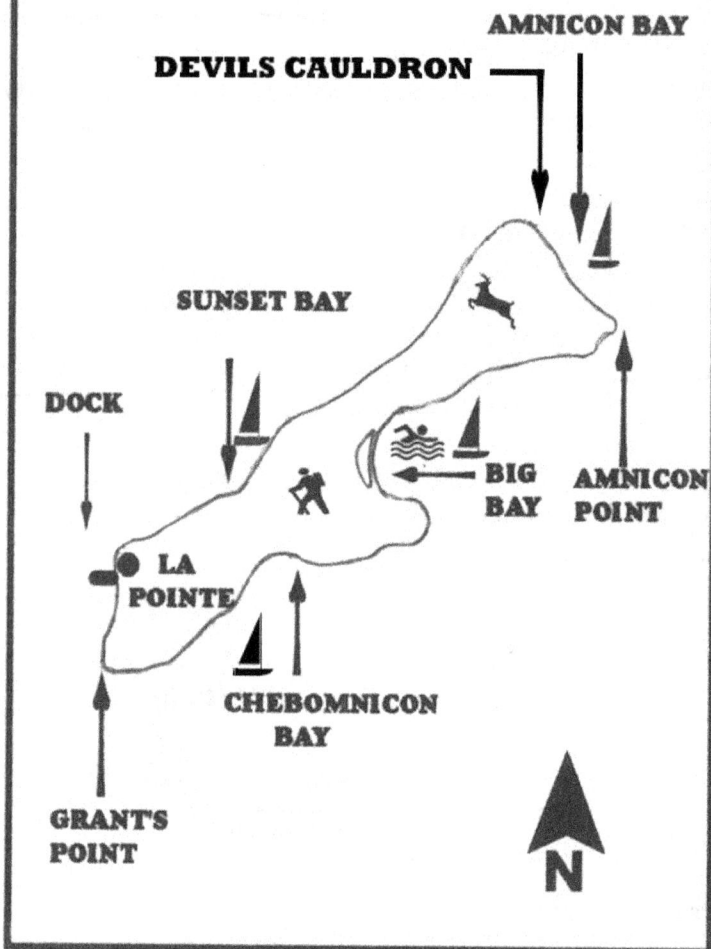

AMNICON BAY

DEVILS CAULDRON

SUNSET BAY

DOCK

LA POINTE

BIG BAY

AMNICON POINT

CHEBOMNICON BAY

GRANT'S POINT

N

MADELINE
(15,000 ACRES; 14 MILES X 3 MILES)

Largest of the Apostle Islands, Madeline was not included in the Apostle Islands National Lakeshore due to the extent of private ownership and commercial development on the island. The island has 45 miles of roads—the only island in the Apostles having them. The island has a rich and varied history, beginning with early Indian activity and continuing into the 17th century as an important outpost of French exploration and fur trading. La Pointe, a town originally located at Grant's Point, is the oldest European settlement in Wisconsin. A museum located just off the dock should be visited to appreciate the rich history of the island.

Madeline has a major dock, a marina, a golf course and a main street in La Pointe containing several commercial establishments. Bears and a plentiful number of deer are found on the island. Madeline's year-round community of about 200 swells to 2500 during the summer. The island is reached by a ferry from Bayfield. (An island map can be obtained from the ferry operator). Previously bearing the Indian name for the golden-breasted woodpecker, the island received its modern name from the daughter of the Indian chief White Crane, when she converted to Christianity.

Public Docks

Although there are no spaces for private boats at the island's main dock it can be used to drop off and pick up boat passengers. The Madeline Island Yacht Club Marina, a short distance south of the main dock, has transient slips.

Trail System

Big Bay State Park, which occupies a significant part of the middle of the island, has an extensive trail system. A brochure, available at the park entrance, contains a map of the trail system. An entrance fee is required.

Toilet Facilities

Public toilet facilities are available in both the Big Bay State Park and the Big Bay Town Park.

Water Availability

Yes

Points of Interest

In addition to the museum and other La Pointe attractions, an outstanding scenic view of an island-studded lagoon can be found atop a bluff near the Big Bay Town Park picnic area at the north end of Big Bay (see page 73).

The Devils Cauldron is located north of Amnicon Bay near the northeast tip of Madeline Island. This large cove set amidst rocky cliffs produces swirling waters and crashing waves under windy conditions, especially those coming from the northeast.

Camping Sites

The Big Bay State Park has an extensive group of camping sites. The Big Bay Town Park also has many sites available. See the reference section for reservation information for these sites.

Beaches

Big Bay State Park has one of the nicest beaches in the Apostles, stretching about two miles along the island's southern shore. This beach also is accessible at the Big Bay Town Park. Although large beaches are found in other bays of the island access to them is restricted since much of the shore property outside Big Bay State Park is under private ownership.

Nautical Cautions

Stay south of the buoy off Grant's Point on Madeline Island as the water between the buoy and the island is shallow. The buoy is over a ½ mile off Grant's Point and can be easily missed. Stay well off the shore when passing Amnicon Point at the northeast corner of Madeline Island.

Anchorages(Prevailing/Forecasted Winds)

Big Bay
 (S, SW, W, NW, N, NE)
Open to the lake

Amnicon Bay
 (S, SW, W)
Open to the lake

Chebomnicon Bay
 (W, NW, N, NE)
Open to the lake

Sunset Bay
 (E, SE, S)

Area south of City Dock
 (NE, E, SE)

Lat/Lon Coordinates

Big Bay Beach	N46°48.7'
	W90°40.3'
Amnicon Bay Beach	N46°51.6'
	W90°35.2'
Chebomnicon Bay Beach	N46°47.0'
	W90°43.0'
Sunset Bay Beach	N46°48.3'
	W90°44.0'
Yacht Club Marina	N46°46.4'
	W90°47.1'
La Pointe Dock	N46°47.0'
	W90°47.7'
Buoy off Grant's Point	N46°45.0'
	W90°48.0'
Devils Cauldron	N46°52.4'
	W90°36.1'

MADELINE ISLAND LAGOON

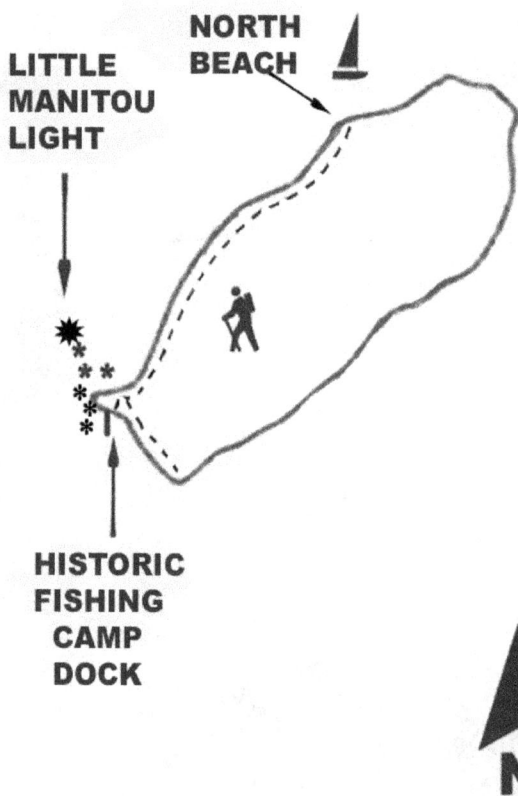

MANITOU

LITTLE
MANITOU
LIGHT

NORTH
BEACH

HISTORIC
FISHING
CAMP
DOCK

N

74

MANITOU
(1400 ACRES; 2 ½ MILES X 1 MILE)

This low-lying island is heavily forested and contains an historic fishing camp.

The island's name is of Indian derivation and means "spirit".

Public Docks
The historic fishing camp is serviced by a dock that is surrounded by boulder-strewn waters.

Campsites
There is one campsite located about 2/3^{rds} of the way up the island's north side.

Trail System
A 1-½ mile trail follows the western shoreline from the fishing camp near the south end of the island to the campsite. There is another short trail from the fishing camp to the island's southwest corner, the site of a historic Indian campsite.

Toilet Facilities
There is a vault toilet off the dock.

Water Availability
None

Points of Interest
The fishing camp, inactive for many years, is a collection of buildings at the island's south end. See page 77.

Beaches

There is a beach on the island's northwest corner adjacent to the camping site.

Nautical Cautions

Use caution when approaching the dock area on Manitou Island as there are rocks in the area. Bear west of Little Manitou Light when rounding the southern end of Manitou Island. One of the most dangerous areas in the islands is the area between the Little Manitou Light and Manitou Island. It is shallow and strewn with boulders and rocks just below the water's surface. Many an unsuspecting sailor has blundered into this area as the distance between Little Manitou Light and Manitou Island is about a half mile.

Anchorages(Prevailing/Forecasted Winds)

Off the beach on the northwest corner
  (E, SE, S)

Lat/Lon Coordinates

Fishing camp dock	N46°57.3'
	W90°40.8'
North beach	N46°58.7'
	W90°39.5'
Little Manitou Light	N46°57.7'
	W90°41.2'

MANITOU ISLAND FISH CAMP

MICHIGAN

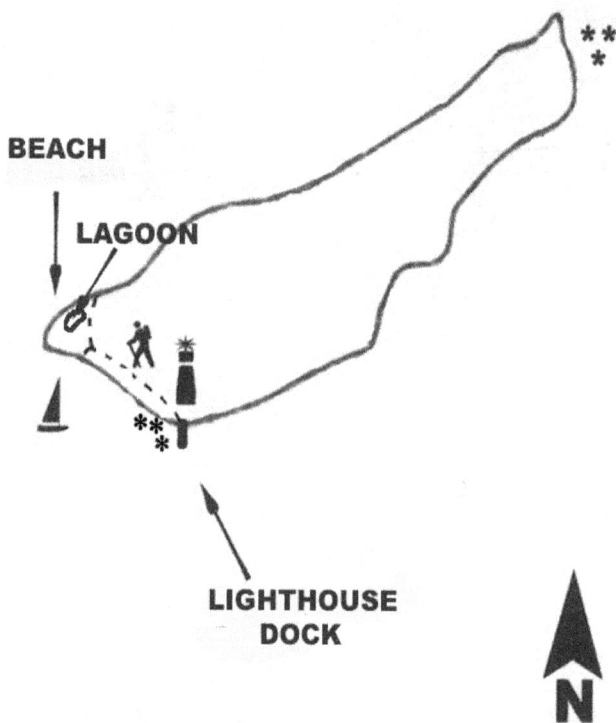

BEACH

LAGOON

LIGHTHOUSE
DOCK

N

MICHIGAN
(1600 ACRES; 3 ½ MILES X 1 ¼ MILES)

The lake bottom drops off sharply from the island's western point reaching a depth of 250 feet only a half mile from shore. The island was named after the nearby state, 21 miles to the south.

Lighthouses
There are two lighthouses located on the lighthouse grounds—mere yards from each other. The shorter lighthouse was built on the island in 1857 in error, being meant for Long Island. It was inactive until 1869, when it was refurbished. The taller lighthouse was built in 1929. The Fresnel lens, which served both lighthouses, is now located in the Apostle Islands National Lakeshore Headquarters building in Bayfield.

Public Docks
There is a dock on the southwest corner of the island from which a 123-step staircase goes up to the lighthouse grounds. Approach the dock carefully as the area leading to it is boulder-strewn and tends to fill with sand due to wave action.

Trail System
A one-mile trail leads from the lighthouse complex to the sand beach at the island's western end. At the west end of the trail there is a side trail that leads to a large lagoon, about a ½ mile away.

Toilet Facilities
There is a vault toilet on the lighthouse grounds.

Water Availability
None

Campsites
There is one campsite in the vicinity where the trail to the lighthouse begins at the beach area on the west end of the island.

Beaches
This island has a large, beautiful sand beach at its western end that extends some distance along its southern and northern shores.

Nautical Cautions
In addition to the previous caution regarding the approach to the dock be sure to avoid the area off the east end of the island facing Gull Island, as it is very shallow and boulder-strewn.

Anchorages(Prevailing/Forecasted Winds)
Off the beach on the southwest corner
  (N, NE, E)
Open to the lake

Lat/Lon Coordinates

Beach at west end	N46°52.6'
	W90°31.2'
Dock leading to lighthouses	N46°52.1'
	W90°29.9'

DEVILS ISLAND LIGHTHOUSE

NORTH TWIN

ROCK
LEDGES →

ROCK
LEDGES ←

SMALL
BEACH
AREAS →

N

NORTH TWIN
(200 ACRES; 1 ¼ MILES x ¼ MILE)

Despite their names the "Twin" islands, North and South, are dissimilar. The island most closely resembling North Twin is Devils, due west of it. Both Devils and North Twin have boreal forests. Unlike Devils Island, however, there are no sea caves on North Twin. Until very recent times the island was known as Brownstone Island, which is more descriptive of its principal feature, brownstone ledges along much of its shore. This island was one of the few to escape extensive cutting during the lumbering period, due to its distance from the mainland, difficulty in gaining access, and its meager pickings—it simply wasn't worth the effort. The island has no trails. Only remote backcountry camping is allowed since there are no campsites available. The island is preserved as an example of a pristine Apostle Island, although until very recently, there was a summer home built by its previous owner at its northern end. Access to the island is difficult and should only be attempted on a calm day or on the leeward side of the island, by approaching the rock ledges that are available.

Public Docks
None

Trail System
None

Toilet Facilities
None

Water Availability
None

Camping Sites
None

Beaches
There are a few meager beach areas studded with rocks near the southwest corner that allow the beaching of a dinghy.

Nautical Cautions
Avoid the shoal extending from the southern end of the island.

Anchorages
None

Lat/Lon Coordinates

Rock ledges on northwest side   N47°04.6'
W90°35.5'

Rock ledges on northeast side   N47°04.4'
W90°34.9'

Area of small beaches   N47°03.9'
W90°35.6'

LONG ISLAND SHOWING ATTACHMENT TO MAINLAND

OAK

FORMER SITE OF "HOLE-IN-THE-WALL" SEA ARCH. COLLAPSED IN 2010

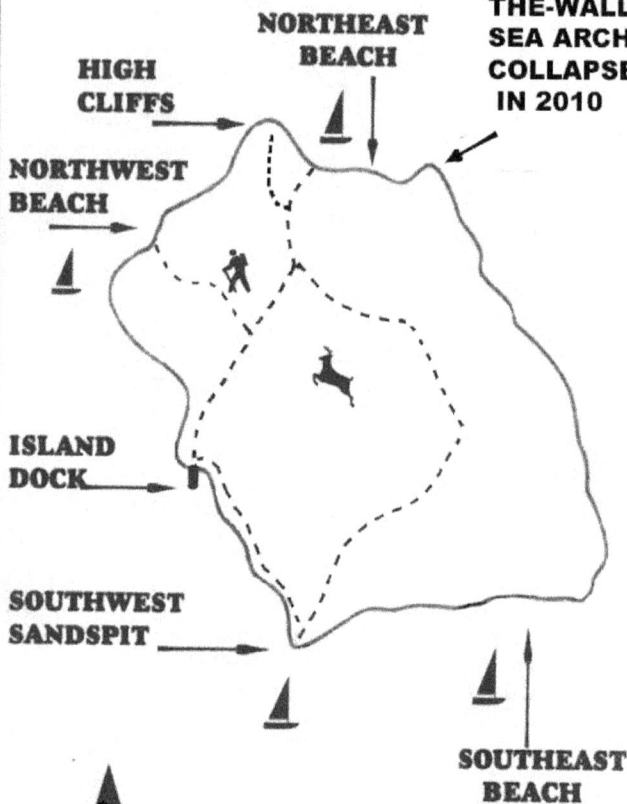

NORTHEAST BEACH

HIGH CLIFFS

NORTHWEST BEACH

ISLAND DOCK

SOUTHWEST SANDSPIT

SOUTHEAST BEACH

N

OAK
(5000 ACRES; 4 MILES X 3 MILES)

Fourth largest and tallest of the islands, rising 500 feet above the lake, Oak was one of the two original Apostle Islands, when the lake level was much higher. It is one of the most recognizable landmarks in the islands due to its height. Oak Island is a rugged, heavily forested island, with many deep ravines. Oak trees were prevalent at one time, providing the basis for the island's name, and can still be found throughout the island. During the time that lumbering took place on the island, men and horses lost their lives traversing the steep sides of the island's ravines hauling logs. Bears and deer inhabit the island.

Public Docks
There is a dock midway up the island's west side.

Trail System
The island's 12 mile trail network can be accessed from the dock on the island's west side. One of the trails runs down to the beach on the far south end and is a comparatively easy hike while the other heads north into the higher elevations, rising 200 feet above the lake. An ancient beach line is crossed on this northern trail. The north trail branches out into several directions—the one that heads due north terminates on an overlook bluff with a beautiful view of the lake and the surrounding islands. Hikers must be in reasonable shape for this hike as the round trip is almost seven miles.

Toilet Facilities
There are vault toilets at all campsites, including one at the dock.

Water Availability
None

Points of Interest
One of the most scenic spots in the islands is located at the water's edge on the island's northern shore—its high cliffs. Waterfalls are sometimes seen along the island's eastern shore, after a period of rain. The Hole in the Wall sea arch, one of the island's former attractions, collapsed in 2010. About a mile and a half south of the island's sandspit is a red buoy marking the edge of deep water for ships making the West Channel passage from the lake to Chequamegon Bay.

Camping Sites
There are six individual campsites and two group campsites spread out over the island. Contact the Park Service for information regarding their locations.

Beaches
Four large beaches are found on the island—on the northwest, southwest, northeast and southeast sides.

Nautical Cautions
Beware of a shoal extending out from western edge of the island about 200 yards.

Anchorages(Prevailing/Forecasted Winds)
Off northeast beach
  (S, SW, W, NW)
Open to the lake

Off southeast beach
  (NW, N, NE)

Off southwest beach
  (NW, N, NE)

 Off northwest beach
  (E, SE, S)
Open to the lake

Lat/Lon Coordinates

Island dock	N46°55.7' W90°45.4'
Southwest sandspit/beach	N46°54.7' W90°44.3'
Northwest beach	N46°57.2' W90°45.6'
Southeast beach	N46°54.9' W90°42.0'
Northeast beach	N46°57.7' W90°43.5'
Former site of Hole In The Wall Sea Arch (Collapsed in 2010)	N46°57.7' W90°42.8'
High cliffs	N46°57.9' W90°44.5'
Red navigational buoy (Marking West Channel Route)	N46°53.7' W90°44.8'

OTTER

MIDPOINT OF
GULL NESTING AREA

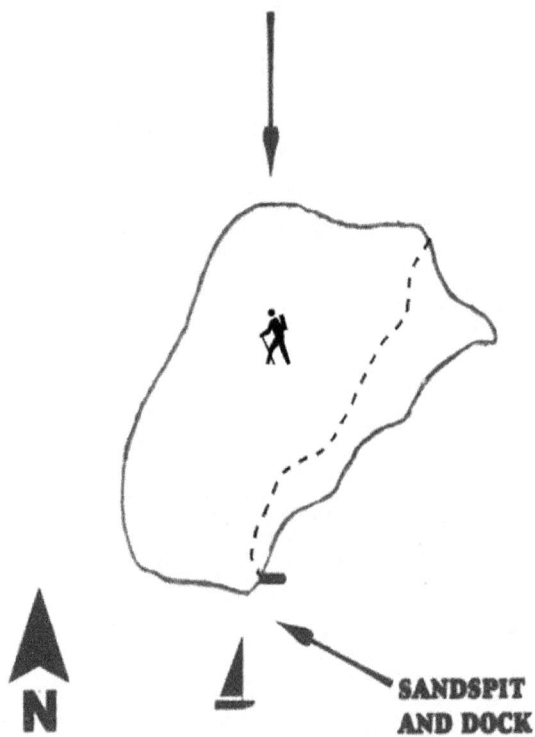

N

SANDSPIT
AND DOCK

OTTER
(1300 ACRES; 2 MILES X 1 ½ MILES)

This heavily forested island is best known for the 1960 Boy Scouts Camporee of almost 1500 scouts that was held on it. The island had been logged over a few years earlier and the scouts were able to set up campsites throughout the island, using the logging roads that were still available. Despite its name there are few otters seen along its shores today.

There is a herring gull nesting site approximately one mile long on the northwest shore of the island and boaters are prohibited from approaching closer than 500 feet from this portion of the shore during the period May 15th to September 1st.

Waterfalls can sometimes be seen on the northern side of the island, after a period of rain.

Public Docks
There is a dock in the vicinity of the sandspit at the southeast end of the island.

Trail System
A trail leads from the sandspit sloping gradually upward about 140 feet and then down to the northeast corner of the island.

Toilet Facilities
There is a vault toilet near the dock.

Water Availability
None

Campsites

There is one campsite in the vicinity of the dock.

Beaches

There is a sandspit located at the far southeast corner of the island.

Nautical Cautions

The passage between Rocky and Otter is quite shallow near Rocky's shore. Be very careful when coming around the northeast corner of Otter Island, staying well offshore, as there is a rocky area extending out from the island.

Anchorages(Prevailing/Forecasted Winds)

Sandbar off the sandspit.
(W, NW, N)
Open to the lake

Lat/Lon Coordinates

Sandspit and dock	N46°59.0' W90°41.6'
Midpoint of gull nesting area	N47°00.6' W90°41.8'

LITTLE MANITOU WITH CORMORANTS

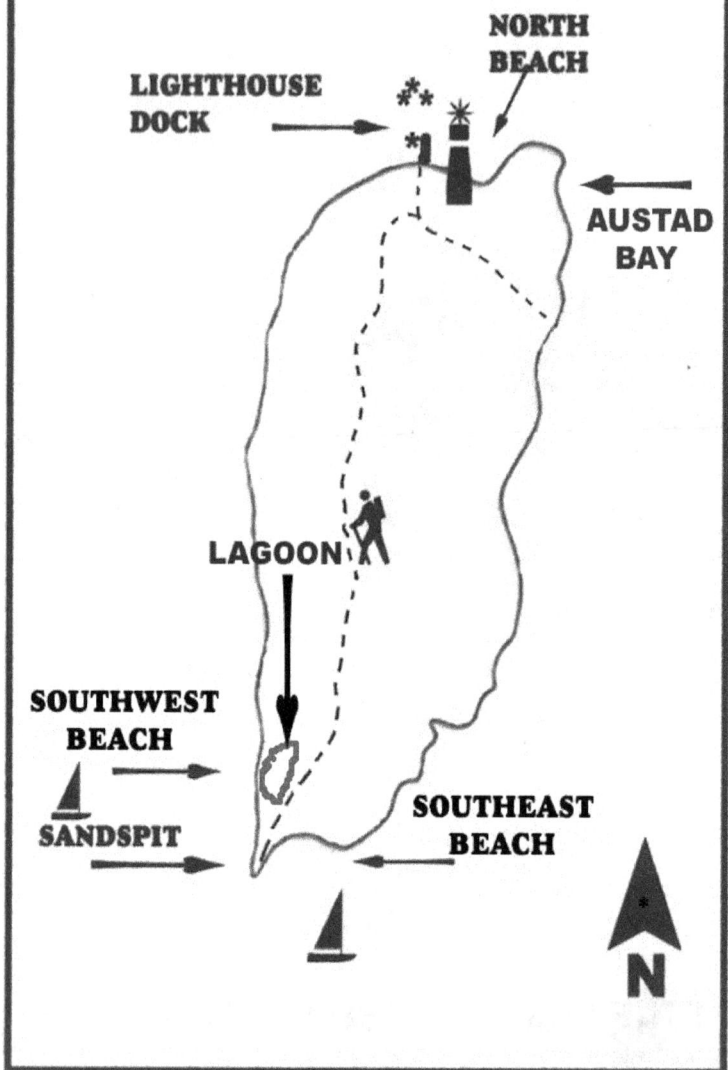

OUTER

NORTH
BEACH

LIGHTHOUSE
DOCK

AUSTAD
BAY

LAGOON

SOUTHWEST
BEACH

SANDSPIT

SOUTHEAST
BEACH

N

OUTER
(8000 ACRES; 6 ¼ MILES X 2 ½ MILES)

The third largest island, after Madeline and Stockton, Outer Island is heavily forested. As the name implies, it is an island on the outer limit of the Apostles, standing like a sentinel, facing the open lake.

Lighthouse
There is a lighthouse, constructed in 1874, located at the island's northern end in the vicinity of the dock. Inexplicably, the hand-crafted Fresnel lens, which sent out its light for many years, was dumped into a Duluth area landfill when this lighthouse was converted to electric light.

Public Docks
Although there is a dock at its northern end leading to a stairway of 98 steps up to a lighthouse, it can only be approached when waters are very calm and only with shallow draft boats.

Trail System
A hiking trail over mostly level ground follows an old railroad bed up the center of the island from the sandspit at the island's southern end to the lighthouse. There is a side trail from the lighthouse leading to the eastern side of the island. Making the hike from the sandspit to the lighthouse and back covers 15 miles—making it a test for only a well-conditioned hiker.

Toilet Facilities
There is a vault toilet on the lighthouse grounds and another near the camping site at the south end of the island.

Water Availability
None

Camping Sites
There is one campsite located off the large sandspit at the south end of the island.

Points of Interest
There is a large lagoon at the northwest end of the sandspit that has shown beaver activity.

Beaches
There is a large, beautiful sandspit at the southern end of the island with beaches extending up both the east and west sides over a mile. There also is a small beach east of the dock on the north end of the island facing the lake—with the boulder hazard mentioned below.

Nautical Cautions
Beware of some old pilings extending out from the western shore about a ½ mile north of the sandspit. Pond nets are sometimes set by commercial fisherman off the sandspit. Boulders litter the shore and the waters surrounding the lighthouse dock at the island's north end making docking hazardous for sailboats or other deep draft vessels. Exposure to the open lake can create wavy conditions or swells that make docking by any boat dangerous.

Anchorages(Prevailing/Forecasted Winds)

Off the southeast beach
 (W, NW, N)
Open to the lake

Off the southwest beach
 (NE, E, SE)
Open to the lake

An anchorage off the beach at the north end is possible but not recommended due to the boulder hazard and exposure to the open lake.

Lat/Lon Coordinates

Sandspit at south end	N46°59.2' W90°28.2'
Southeast beach	N46°59.7' W90°27.4'
Southwest beach	N46°59.8' W90°28.3'
Dock at north end	N47°04.8' W90°25.0'
Beach on north end	N47°04.7' W90°24.7'

RASPBERRY

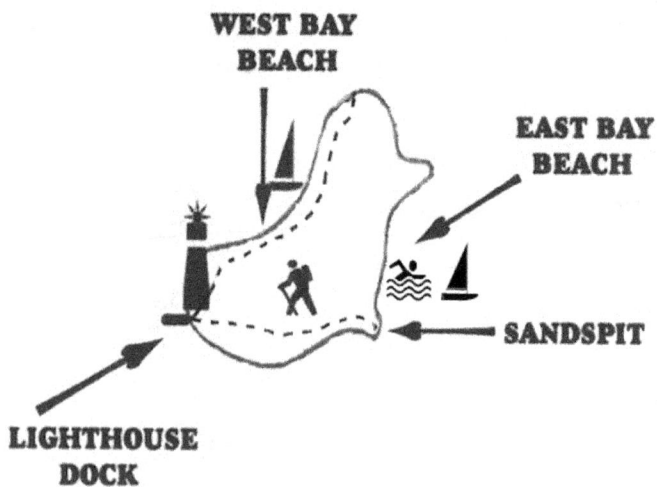

WEST BAY
BEACH

EAST BAY
BEACH

SANDSPIT

LIGHTHOUSE
DOCK

N

98

RASPBERRY
(300 ACRES; 1 MILE x ½ MILE)

There is a beautiful sheltered bay on this island's eastern shore, north of a sandspit, which is a prized anchorage for boats. The island escaped the woodman's axe since the entire island was considered exempt under the lighthouse forest reservation policy, which set aside a portion of the forest surrounding a lighthouse for the keeper's use.

The island apparently received its name due to its proximity to Raspberry Bay and the Raspberry River, which are across from the island, on the mainland.

Less than a half mile west of the lighthouse dock is a green navigational buoy marking the deep water passage for large ships transiting the West Channel from the lake to Chequamegon Bay.

Lighthouse
This island contains one of the most beautiful lighthouse complexes in the Apostles at its south-western end. The original lighthouse, constructed in 1863, about the time the Gettysburg battle was fought during the Civil War, no longer stands, although some of its original foundation still exists. The Fresnel lens was removed from the lighthouse and is now on display in the Madeline Island Museum. There is a staircase leading up from the dock area to the lighthouse grounds, which contains a large flower garden. Extensive renovation of the lighthouse complex was undertaken during 2005 and 2006 (see page 53). A park ranger is on duty during the summer and conducts tours of the lighthouse for a fee.

Public Docks

There is a dock area, consisting of two piers, in front of the lighthouse.

Trail System

A trail leads east from the lighthouse complex to the sandspit, which is about a ½ mile away. Another trail leads from the lighthouse grounds north to an overlook, about a mile distant, from which the Sand Island lighthouse can be seen—a duty that was once required of the Raspberry Island lighthouse keepers. This trail is not maintained and requires climbing over and ducking under fallen trees.

Toilet Facilities

There is a vault toilet on the lighthouse grounds and another at the sandspit area.

Water Availability

None

Campsites

None

Beaches

There two beaches—one in the sheltered bay on the island's eastern shore and another in the bay on the island's west side.

Nautical Cautions

None

Anchorages(Prevailing/Forecasted Winds)

Bay north of the sandspit on east side
  (SW, W, NW, N)

Bay on west side
  (NE, E, SE, S)
Open to the lake

Raspberry Bay (on mainland)
  (SE, S, SW, W, NW)
Open to the lake

Lat/Lon Coordinates

Lighthouse dock	**N46°58.2'**
	W90°48.4'
Sandspit on east side	**N46°58.4'**
	W90°47.3'
Green navigational buoy	**N46°58.2'**
(Marking West Channel Route)	**W90°48.5'**
West bay	**N46°58.6'**
	W90°48.0'
Raspberry Bay	**N46°56.2'**
(on mainland)	**W90°49.3'**

ROCKY

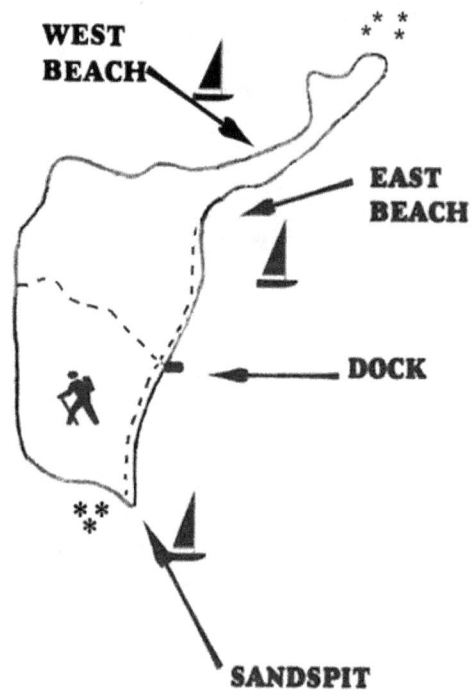

WEST
BEACH

EAST
BEACH

DOCK

SANDSPIT

N

ROCKY
(1100 ACRES; 2 MILES X 1 MILE)

One of the strangest shaped islands in the Apostles, Rocky has a northern appendage shaped somewhat like a chicken's neck and head and a southern portion resembling a chicken's body. The island has a colorful past, having been the site of a large Norwegian fishing community dating back to the early 1930s.

Public Docks
There is a public dock on the east side about a mile north of the sandspit at the southern end.

Trail System
A trail leads from the dock to an overlook on the west side of the island, about a mile distant. Trails also follow the shore, both north and south, from the dock. The trail that leads north goes to the historic fishing community—a cluster of docks and cabins, some of which are privately occupied.   The trail going south ends at the sandspit.

Toilet Facilities
There are vault toilets at all campsites and at the dock.

Water Availability
None

Campsites
There are seven campsites spread out from the dock toward the sandspit at the south end of the island.

Beaches

In addition to the sandspit on the southeast side there is a long beach running along the east side of the island's "neck" and another on the west side.

Nautical Cautions

As the island's name implies, there are rocky shores on the south end of the island and off the northern tip. Stay well off the shore when passing these points. Caution should be exercised transiting through the shallow northern channel between Rocky and South Twin, especially in years of low water levels. Sailboats and other similar deep draft vessels should avoid this area. When rounding Rocky's southern edge stay well off shore as it is shallow a significant distance off the shore.

Anchorages(Prevailing/Forecasted Winds)

Off the beach and sandspit on east side
  (SW, W, NW, N)

Off the beach on west side
  (NE, E, SE, S, SW)
Open to the lake

Lat/Lon Coordinates

Public dock	N47°01.7'/W90°40.4'
Sandspit at southern end	N47°01.1'/W90°40.7'
Beach on east side	N47°02.4'/W90°40.0'
Beach on west side	N47°02.9'/W90°40.0'

ROCKY ISLAND LOOKING SOUTH

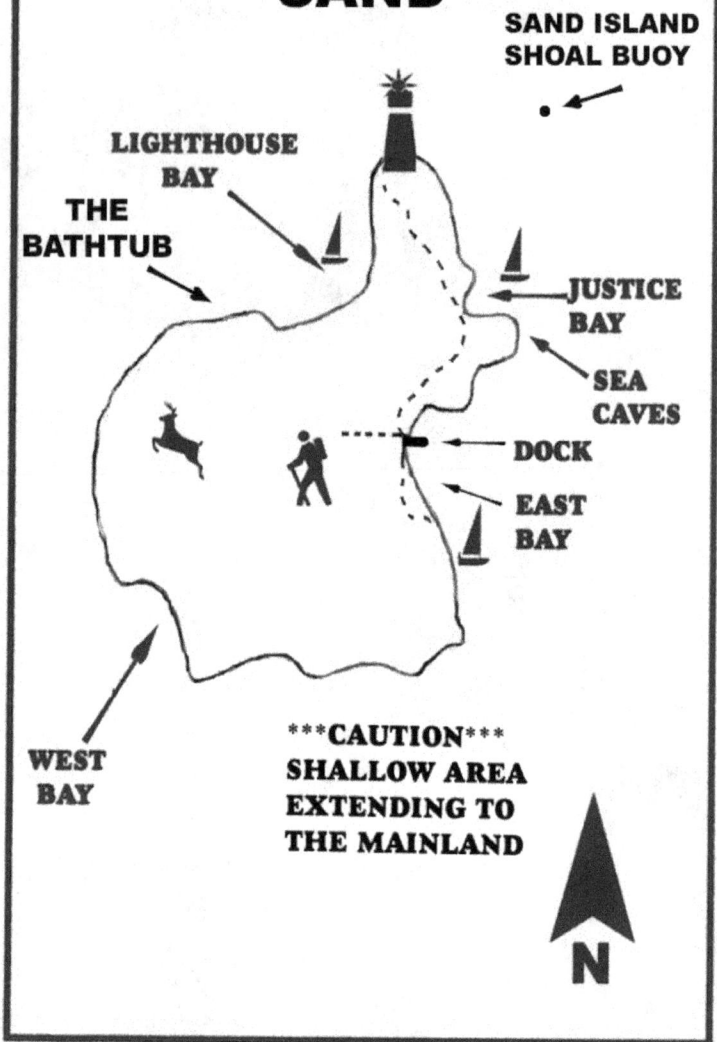

SAND

SAND ISLAND SHOAL BUOY

LIGHTHOUSE BAY

THE BATHTUB

JUSTICE BAY

SEA CAVES

DOCK

EAST BAY

WEST BAY

CAUTION
SHALLOW AREA
EXTENDING TO
THE MAINLAND

N

SAND
(2900 ACRES; 3 MILES X 3 MILES)

This is the only one of the Apostle Islands beside Madeline to have had a substantial population in the past. At one time, the small village of Shaw, composed primarily of Norwegian immigrants, was located on it. The island apparently received its name due to its proximity to the Sand River and Sand Bay located on the mainland. It is a heavily forested island that has very little elevation, making it an ideal breeding ground for mosquitoes after a period of rain.

A tragic event took place in September 1905, when the steamer *Sevona* broke up on Sand Island Shoal during a terrible storm. The captain and most of the crew were lost and their bodies washed ashore in Justice and East Bays.

Lighthouse
Located at the island's northern tip, the Sand Island lighthouse was built in 1881 and is judged by many to be the most beautiful in the islands (see page 41). It is constructed of stone and has a house attached. The shoreline at the foot of the lighthouse grounds, which is reached by a stairway, is a rocky ledge that is composed of sandstone nearly a billion years old.

Public Docks
There is a public dock at East Bay. Docks on the island's southeast and west sides are private. The dock at Little Sand Bay, southeast of Sand Island, is located on a twelve-mile stretch of mainland included in the National Lakeshore.

Trail System

There are trails from the dock at East Bay to the lighthouse at the north end of the island, one to the former site of Shaw and another that goes directly west to some campsites.

Toilet Facilities

There is vault toilet off the dock at East Bay and one on the lighthouse grounds.

Water Availability

In the clearing off the dock at East Bay.

Points of Interest

From the waters offshore or an anchorage in Justice Bay, boaters can see the sea caves and sea stacks to the southeast under Swallow Point (see page 113). The Bathtub, located about one mile west of Lighthouse Bay, is a small cove that generates swirling waters, waves and strong currents during windy conditions, especially those coming from the north, northeast and northwest. Note cautionary warning on page 27 regarding entry into the sea caves.

Campsites

There are two individual and two group campsites in the vicinity of the East Bay dock, and one campsite at the end of Lighthouse Bay.

Beaches

Beaches are found in the island's four bays.

Nautical Cautions

If attempting to view the south end of the island or anchor in West Bay (not recommended), an approach to these areas should be made along the west side of the island as the area between the southeast corner of the island and the mainland is shallow. Stay well away from the shore when making the transit around the west side of the island. Be cautious when approaching the dock at East Bay, as this bay is shallow. Don't approach the lighthouse point too closely due to ledges and boulders.

Anchorages
East Bay
  (SW, W, NW, N)

Justice Bay
  (S, SW, W, NW)
Open to the lake

Lighthouse Bay
  (NE, E, SE, S, SW)
Open to the lake

Lat/Lon Coordinates

East Bay Dock	**N46°58.9'/ W90°55.7'**
Justice Bay	**N46°59.5'/ W90°55.5'**
Swallow Point Sea Caves	**N46°59.4'/ W90°55.3'**
Lighthouse	**N47°00.3'/ W90°56.3'**
West Bay	**N46°58.2'/ W90°58.5'**
Lighthouse Bay	**N46°59.7'/ W90°56.7'**
Sand Island Shoal Buoy	**N47°00.9'/ W90°54.3'**

SOUTH TWIN

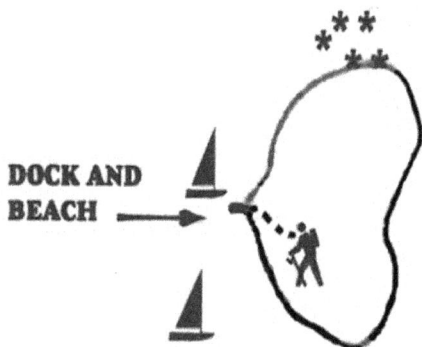

DOCK AND
BEACH →

N

SOUTH TWIN
(400 ACRES; 1 MILE X ¾ MILE)

The area between Rocky and South Twin is a commonly used anchorage in the upper reaches of the Apostles due to the protection the islands provide from most all winds. As noted in the description of North Twin, the two islands designated as "twins" are dissimilar, having little in common. The derivation of their names is not well documented, so one can only assume that their proximity was the only basis.

There is a visitor exhibit structure in the dock area, which contains a labeled collection of various beach stones.

The bottom drops quickly off the southwest corner of the island, which can make anchorages there some-what precarious if the wind shifts.

Public Docks
There is a dock midway up the west side of the island.

Trail System
A short trail from the dock area leads to a large overgrown clearing to the southeast, marking the airstrip of the island's former owner.

Toilet Facilities
There is a vault toilet adjacent to the dock.

Water Availability
None

Camping Sites

There are four campsites off the beach in the dock area.

Beaches

There is a beach area located on the island's west side in the vicinity of the dock.

Nautical Cautions

The northern shore of South Twin is studded with rocks near the surface and should be avoided. Caution should be exercised transiting through the shallow northern channel between Rocky and South Twin, especially in years of low water levels. Sailboats and other similar deep draft vessels should avoid this area.

Anchorages(Prevailing/Forecasted Winds)

North and south of the dock.
  (NW, N, NE, E, SE)

Lat/Lon Coordinates

Island dock and beach   N47°02.0'
                          W90°39.2'

SAND ISLAND SWALLOW POINT SEA CAVES

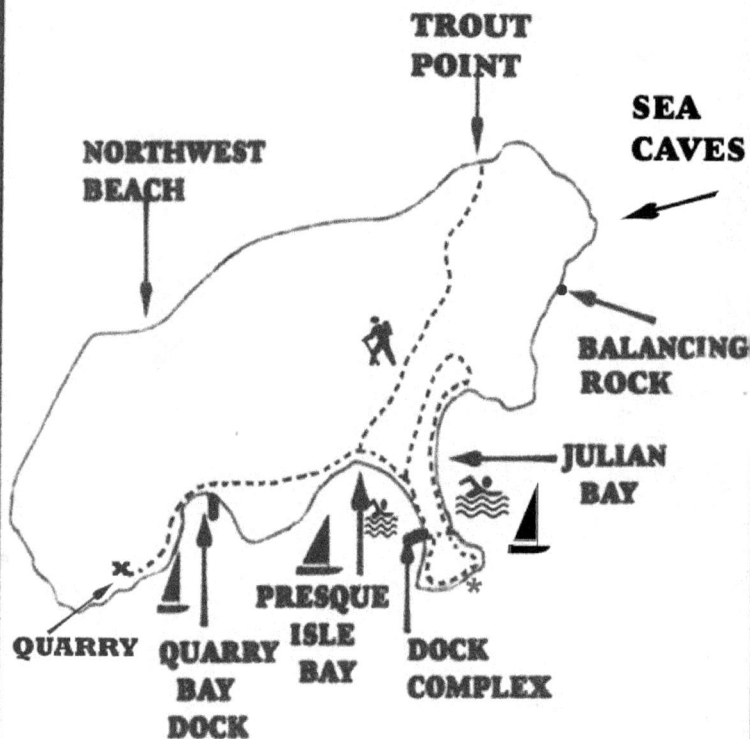

STOCKTON

TROUT POINT

SEA CAVES

NORTHWEST BEACH

BALANCING ROCK

JULIAN BAY

QUARRY

QUARRY BAY DOCK

PRESQUE ISLE BAY

DOCK COMPLEX

N

STOCKTON
(10,000 ACRES; 7 ¼ MILES X 2 ½ MILES)

The second largest of the Apostle Islands, Stockton Island, known for its large bear population, is the most visited island in the National Lakeshore. After extensive research local historian Marjory Benton determined that the basis for the island's name, formerly Presque Isle, was General John Stockton, a pioneer resident of Mt. Clemons, Michigan, who apparently never visited the island. Stockton's name was assigned to the island on a map that was attached to a report to Congress in 1845. At the time Stockton was U. S. Superintendent, Lake Superior Mines.

Public Docks

There is a large dock on the west side of Presque Isle Point with an adjoining visitor's center. All moorings must be made on the inside portion due to the rock breakwater surrounding the outside portion of the dock. Most vessels having a deep draft should anchor in Presque Isle Bay as the dock area is too shallow. There is also a dock at Quarry Bay.

Trail System

There is a well-maintained trail system on the island. A short ¼ mile trail leads from the dock complex to Julian Bay on the other side of Presque Isle Point. Shortly before reaching Julian Bay there is an overlook that gives a magnificent view of a bog that extends over a mile. By following the Julian Bay beach north, hikers will hook up with the Tombolo Trail that leads around the bog back to the dock. If taking this trail in mid-July to mid-August, hikers can pick blueberries—assuming, of course, that the bears haven't gotten to them first. Another trail leads west

115

from the dock, along a string of camping sites, past Quarry Bay, to the abandoned brownstone quarries on the southwest corner of the island. Another trail follows the shore around Presque Isle Point from the dock to Julian Bay, which has a magnificent expanse of beach. There is also a trail that goes right up through the center of the island to Trout Point, the site of an old logging camp, on the island's north shore.

Toilet Facilities

There are toilet facilities adjacent to the visitor center at Presque Isle Bay and a vault toilet is located off the dock in Quarry Bay. Vault toilets are also available at the campsites.

Water Availability

Water is available in the visitor center area in Presque Isle Bay.

Points of Interest

A small area of sea caves is found on the island's eastern shore, north of a rock column named Balancing Rock. Abandoned brownstone quarries are located on the southwest end of the island and can be reached by the existing trails.

Camping Sites

There are nineteen prime individual campsites overlooking Presque Isle Bay stretching from the dock area about a mile to the north, plus additional sites at Quarry Bay and Trout Point. There are two group campsites in the vicinity of Quarry Bay.

Beaches

Stockton has three picturesque bays with beaches, two on the south side, west of Presque Isle Point (Presque Isle Bay and Quarry Bay) and one on the east side (Julian Bay). The Julian Bay beach is considered one of the finest in the islands (see page119). There also is a beach on the northwest side of the island.

Nautical Cautions

Large rocks acting as a breakwater line the outside portion of the Stockton Island Presque Isle dock. Do not approach the left side of the outside portion too closely as there are rocks from an abandoned crib close to the surface.

Use caution when anchoring in the northern portion of Presque Isle Bay as it has an extensive shallow area.

Stay well off shore (200+ yards) when rounding Presque Isle Point of Stockton Island as some areas are hazardous, with large boulders and rock ledges near the surface.

Anchorages(Prevailing/Forecasted Winds)

Presque Isle Bay
  (NW, N, NE, E, SE)

Quarry Bay
  (W, NW, N, NE, E)

Julian Bay
  (SW, W, NW, N)
Open to the lake

Lat/Lon Coordinates

Dock Complex	**N46°54.8'**
	W90°33.2'
Presque Isle Bay	**N46°55.0'**
	W90°33.4'
Julian Bay	**N46°55.5'**
	W90°32.5'
Quarry Bay Dock	**N46°55.1'**
	W90°36.4'
Trout Point	**N46°58.3'**
	W90°31.7'
Northwest beach	**N46°56.8'**
	W90°37.0'
Balancing Rock/Sea Caves	**N46°56.8'**
	W90°31.0'

STOCKTON ISLAND
PRESQUE ISLE POINT AND JULIAN BAY

119

YORK

NORTH
BEACH

SANDSPIT

N

120

YORK
(300 ACRES; 1 ½ MILES x ¾ MILE)

This island is strangely shaped appearing to be a club with a crooked handle. At one time the island was smaller consisting only of the present island's eastern portion. Within fairly recent times the action of waves produced a sandbar, which joined the original York Island with a smaller island (Rock) to the west. The east end of the island is heavily forested.

The name derivation is believed to be associated with British naval Lt. Henry Bayfield, who named it after his ancestral home in England, in an 1824 survey of the islands.

Public Docks
None. There is a dock at Little Sand Bay, southwest of York Island, located on a twelve-mile stretch of the mainland included in the Apostle Islands National Lakeshore.

Trail System
None

Toilet Facilities
There is a vault toilet adjacent to the campsites.

Water Availability
None

Campsites
There are three campsites off the north beach.

Points of Interest

There is a monument on a bluff off the western edge of the sandspit, constructed by the Allen family, as a tribute to their son and brother, Merlin Raye Allen, a Marine who perished in combat aboard a helicopter during the Vietnam War and was listed as Missing in Action. In February 2013 Allen's remains were recovered in Vietnam and buried on York Island in June of that year. The Allen family, who owned York Island and a portion of the mainland at the time the national park was formed in 1970, deeded two acres of the property that contains the monument and graves of Allen family members to the Town of Russell along with ten acres on the mainland, with the stipulation it would be the final resting place for the Allen family. The two acres owned by the Town of Russell on York Island is the only portion of any island included in the Apostle Islands National Lakeshore that is not owned by the federal government.

Beaches

As one might expect, given the geology of this island, there is an extensive beach along its northern shore. There is also a sandspit beach on the south end of the island that extends under the water as a sand shoal for some distance.

Nautical Cautions

The waters surrounding York Island, especially on the east, northeast, northwest and west ends are studded with boulders, some a considerable distance from the island (150-200 yards). Stay well off shore of these areas. The shoal from the sandspit extends a significant distance from the shore.

Anchorages(Prevailing/Forecasted Winds)

Off the beach on the northern side
  (SE, S, SW, W)
Open to the lake

West of the sandspit shoal at southern end
  (NW, N,NE)

Lat/Lon Coordinates

North side beach	N46°59.3' W90°52.0'
Sandspit at south end	N46°58.4' W90°51.5'
Dock at Little Sand Bay (on mainland)	N46°57.0' W90°53.5'

SOURCES FOR ADDITIONAL INFORMATION

Apostle Islands

Holzhueter, John O., *Madeline Island and the Chequamegon Region,* Madison: The State Historical Society of Wisconsin, 1986. A historical review of Madeline Island and the surrounding region.

National Park Service, *A Guide to Apostle Islands National Lakeshore,* Washington: Department of Publications, U. S. Department of the Interior, 1988. Official National Park Handbook for the Apostle Islands National Lakeshore.

National Park Service, DVD/VHS, *On the Edge of Gichigami—Voices of the Apostle Islands*, Produced by Harper's Ferry Center (20 min).

Newman, Lawrence, *Discovering the Apostle Islands*, South Elgin: Silver Millennium Publications, Inc., 2012. A visitor's guide to the Apostle Islands area containing extensive color photos.

Newman, Lawrence, *Sailing Adventures In The Apostle Islands,* South Elgin: Silver Millennium Publications, Inc., 2011. A cruising guide to the Apostle Islands containing extensive labled color photos.

Rennicke, Jeff, photographs by Layne Kennedy, *Jewels on the Water,* Friends of the Apostle Islands National Lakeshore, 2005. Photographic review of Apostle Islands history—both past and present.

Ross, Hamilton, *La Pointe: Village Outpost on Madeline Island*, Madison: State Historical Society, 2000. History of LaPointe and Madeline Island.

Strzok, Dave, *A Visitor's Guide to the Apostle Islands National Lakeshore,* Ashland: Superior Printing and Specialties, 1999. A comprehensive review of the islands and their history, including useful information for those boating, hiking and camping in the islands.

Dahl, Bonnie, *The Superior Way-A Cruising Guide to Lake Superior*, Duluth: Lake Superior Port Cities Inc., 2001. Includes information on the Apostle Islands.

The Apostle Islands National Lakeshore Head-quarters in Bayfield has an assortment of free brochures describing the more visited islands and several providing useful information on hiking, camping, boating, scuba diving and kayaking activities in the islands. Website: nps.gov/apis

Area Information
Ashland Area Chamber of Commerce
1716 West Lake Shore Drive
Ashland, WI 54806
800-284-9484
715-682-2500
visitashland.com

Bayfield County Tourism
117 E. 6th Street
Washburn, WI 54891
800-472-6338
travelbayfieldcounty.com

Bayfield Chamber of Commerce and Visitors Bureau
42 S. Broad St.
Bayfield, WI 54814
800-447-4094/715-779-3335
bayfield.org

Madeline Island Chamber of Commerce
PO Box 274
LaPointe, WI 54850
888-475-3386
715-747-2801
madelineisland.com

Washburn Area Chamber of Commerce
126 W. Bayfield St.
Washburn, WI 54891
800-253-4495
715-373-5017

<u>Beach Stones</u>
Stensaas, Mark Sparky, Illustrated by Kollath, Rick, *Rock Picker's Guide to Lake Superior's North Shore*, Duluth: Kollath-Stensaas Publishing, 2000.

Robinson, Susan, *Is This an Agate?—An Illustrated Guide to Lake Superior's Beach Stones/Michigan*, private printing, no date of publication.

Pellant, Chris, *Rocks and Minerals,* New York: Dorling Kindersley, Inc., 1992. A visual guide to more than 500 rocks and minerals from around the world.

<u>Berries</u>
Lyle, Katie Letcher, *The Wild Berry Book*, Minocqua: Northward Press, Inc., 1994.

Miller, Dorras S., Illustrated by Cherie Hunter Day, *Berry Finder*, Rochester: Nature Study Guild, no date of publication.

<u>Birds</u>
Temple, Stanley A., *Birds of the Apostle Islands,* Hartland, Wisconsin: The Wisconsin Society of Ornithology, Inc., 1985. A survey of the types of birds found on the islands of the Apostle Islands National Lakeshore.

Tekiela, Stan, *Birds of Wisconsin Field Guide*, Cambridge, Minnesota: Adventure Publications, 1999.

Peterson, Roger Tory, *A Field Guide to Birds East of the Rockies*, Boston, New York: Houghton Mifflin Company, 1980.

Birding by the Bay, free pamphlet, available from the Ashland Area Chamber of Commerce.

<u>Boating</u>
Wisconsin Boating Regulations—obtain at marinas and the Apostle Islands National Lakeshore Headquarters in Bayfield. Can also be obtained directly from the Wisconsin Department of Natural Resources, PO Box 7921, Madison, WI 53707

Dodds, Don, *Modern Seamanship,* New York: Lyons and Burford, 1995. Comprehensive and compact guide for boaters, covering in detail the use of such labor-saving technological advances as GPS and traditional seamanship skills.

Murrant, Jim, *The Boating Bible,* Dobbs Ferry, New York: Sheridan House Inc., 1991. This book, written by a seasoned sailing instructor, instructs the reader in all the skills necessary to be able to sail competently.

Rousmaniere,John, *The Annapolis Book of Seamanship,* New York: Simon and Schuster, 1999, 3rd Edition. The best-selling book in its field, it is used throughout America as a textbook in sailing schools and Power Squadrons.

Chapman Piloting: Seamanship and Boat Handling, New York: Hearst Marine Books, 2006. The 65th edition of this well written and illustrated "gold standard" of seamanship was produced by St. Remy Media with the assistance of several knowledgeable consultants under the direction of Dan Foles.

<u>Camping—National Lakeshore</u>
National Park Service
Apostle Islands National Lakeshore Headquarters
415 Washington Ave
Bayfield, WI 54814
715-779-3397
Camping permits can be obtained in Bayfield, at the National Park Service office in Little Sand Bay and at the islands' docks. Request the brochure "Camping in the Apostle Islands" from the National Park Service.

<u>Campgrounds</u>
Apostle Islands Area Campground
½ mile south of Bayfield on Highway 13 & County J
715-779-5524

Big Bay State Park
Madeline Island
715-747-6425
Reservations must be made through Reserve America
(reserveamerica.com) 888-947-2757

Big Bay Town Park
Madeline Island
1st come/1st served (Fee for use—payable at campground)

Buffalo Bay Campground and Marina
14669 Highway 13
Bayfield, WI 54814
Located in the Village of Red Cliff, 2 ½ miles north of Bayfield
715-779-3743

Dalrymple Campground
1 mile north of Bayfield on Highway 13
1st come/1st served (Fee for use—payable at campground)
Operated by City of Bayfield
cityofbayfield.com

Little Sand Bay Campground
715-779-5233
Operated by Town of Russell

Memorial Park
Washburn, WI
715-373-6174
Operated by Town of Washburn

Point Detour Campground
1st come/1st served (Fee for use—payable at camp-ground)
Operated by National Park Service

West End Park
Washburn, WI
715-373-6174
Operated by Town of Washburn

Camping, Boating and Hiking Supplies
Adventure Vacations
Corner of Main & Middle Roads (Madeline Island)
715-747-2100
www.adv-vac.com

Super Walmart
2500 E. Lakeshore Drive
Ashland, WI 54806
715-682-9699

There are grocery and hardware stores in Bayfield, Washburn and Ashland that carry provisions and supplies for camping, boating and hiking trips.

Charts/Maps
FAA Distribution Division, AVN-530
NOAA Charting Office
Glen Dale, MD, 20769
800-638-8972/301-436-8301
chartmaker.ncd.noaa.gov/staff/charts.htm
Request Nautical Chart #14973 (Apostle Islands)
This chart can also usually be found for sale at stores and marinas in the Bayfield area.

Mapping Specialists
1319 Applegate Road
Madison WI 53713
866-525-2298
www.mappingspecialists.com
Request map of Chequamegon Bay and Apostle Islands. Contains markings of fish refuge areas.

National Geographic Outdoor Recreation Maps
nationalgeographic.com/maps
Request map of Apostle Islands (#235)

Cruise Boats/Water Taxis/Ferry
Apostle Islands Cruises
2 N. Front Street (City Dock)
Bayfield, WI 54814
(715)779-3925/(800)323-7619
www.apostleislandscruises.com

Adventure Vacations
104 Middle Road
La Pointe, WI 54850
Water taxis from Bayfield and La Pointe
715-747-2100
www.adv-vac.com

Nourse's Sport Fishing (Water taxi service also)
100 Yacht Club Drive, end of 3rd St.
Bayfield, WI 54814
866-819-4330/715-779-3253
www.noursesfishing.com

Madeline Island Ferry Line
715-747-2051
madferry.com

Fish of Lake Superior
Bailey, John, *Ultimate Freshwater Fishing*, New York:
DK Publishing, 1998.

Bosanko, Dave, *Fish Of Wisconsin,* Cambridge,
Minnesota: Adventure Publications, 2007

Perich, Shawn, *Fishing Lake Superior*, Duluth: Pfeifer-
Hamilton, 1994.

Fish of the Great Lakes website:
seagrant.wisc.edu/greatlakesfish

Current Wisconsin fishing regulations—obtain at:
Wisconsin Department of Natural Resources
101 S. Webster Street
Madison, WI 53703
608-266-2621
fishingwisconsin.org
Can normally be obtained at local bait shops.

Footprint Identification
Halfpenny, James C., *Scats and Tracks of the Great
Lakes*, Guilford: Morris Book Publishing Company,
2006.

Miller, Doreas, *Track Finder*, Rochester: Nature Study
Guide Publishers, no date of publication.

Friends of the Apostle Islands National Lakeshore/
Apostle Islands Historic Preservation Conservancy
Friends of the Apostle Islands National Lakeshore
PO Box 1574
Bayfield, WI 54814
715-779-3397 Ext. 444
friendsoftheapostleislands.org

Apostle Islands Historic Preservation Conservancy
Mr. Robert Mackreth
500 Woodland Drive
Washburn, WI 54891
715-373-0818
www.bobmackreth.com

Geology

Dotts, Jr., Robert H. and Attig, John W., *Roadside Geology of Wisconsin*, Missoula: Mountain Press Publishing, 2004.

Laberge, Gene L., *Geology of the Lake Superior Region*, Tucson: Geoscience Press, Inc., 1994.

Nuhfer, Edward B., *A Guidebook to the Geology of Lake Superior's National Lakeshore.* Fort Washington: Eastern National, 2004. Book includes poetry by Mary P. Dalles. Detailed exposition on the geologic formations in the Apostle Islands.

Hiking

McKinney, John, *The Joy of Hiking: Hiking the Trailmaster Way*, Berkeley: Wilderness Press, 2005.
National Park Service, *Hiker's Guide to Apostle Islands National Lakeshore,* Edited by Neil Howk, Asst. Chief of Resources Education, Apostle Islands National Lakeshore, Fort Washington: Eastern National, 2001.

Website describing hiking trails in the islands: gorp.com/gorp/resource/us_ns/wi/hik_apo.htm

Inland Sea Society
PO Box 145
Washburn, WI 54891
715-682-8188
inlandsea.org

This organization of kayak enthusiasts has been an active advocate of Lake Superior environmental and cultural issues and is currently pursuing a goal of establishing a 3000-mile waterway trail around Lake Superior. Contact them for a free water trail map.

Kayaks/Canoes
Living Adventure Inc. (kayaks)
88260 State Highway 13
Bayfield WI 54814
715-779-9503/866-779-9503
www.livingadventure.com
Located 2 miles north of Bayfield in Red Cliff

Apostle Islands Kayaks-Madeline Island
715-747-3636
apostleislandskayaks.com

Wilderness Inquiry (kayaks)
33090 Little Sand Bay Rd.
Bayfield, WI 54814
800-728-0719/612-676-9400

Boreal Shores (kayaks)
222 Rittenhouse Ave.
Bayfield, WI 54814
715-779-5500
borealshores.com

Trek & Trail Adventure Outfitters (kayaks)
7 Washington Ave
Bayfield, WI 54814
800-354-8735
715-779-3595
Trek-Trail.com

Bog Lake Outfitters
Canoe and rowboat rentals
Big Bay Town Park, Madeline Island
715-747-2685

Lighthouses
Lighthouse Celebration Cruises
PO Box 990
Bayfield, WI 54814
800-779-4487
lighthousecelebration.com
Held annually in early September.
Visits are made to Apostle Islands lighthouses, where guided tours are available, including Sand, Michigan and Raspberry Islands.

Keeper of the Light
19 Front Street
Bayfield, WI 54814
800-779-4487
keeperofthelight.net
This store stocks a variety of nautical and lighthouse merchandise.

Marinas
Apostle Islands Marina
107 Manypenny St.
Bayfield, WI 54814
715-779-5661/715-779-5505
Monitors Channel 16
Transient slips available
cityofbayfield.com
Lat/Lon coordinates for harbor entrance: N46°48.6'
                                          W90°48.5'

Ashland Marina
Behind the Hotel Chequamegon
At intersection of US 2 and St. Route 13
715-682-7049
Transient slips available
Lat/Lon coordinates for harbor entrance: N46°35.8'
                                           W90°53.8'

Buffalo Bay Marina and Campground
14669 Highway 13
Bayfield, WI 54814
715-779-3743
Located 3 miles north of Bayfield in Town of Red Cliff
Transient slips available
Lat/Lon coordinates for harbor entrance: N46°51.2'
                                          W90°47.2'

Madeline Island Yacht Club Marina
LaPointe, WI 54850
715-747-2655
Monitors Channel 16
Transient slips available
Lat/Lon coordinates for harbor entrance: N46°46.4'
                                           W90°47.1'

Pike's Bay Marina
1-½ miles south of Bayfield on Highway 13
877-841-3900/715-779-3900
pikesbaymarina.com
Transient slips available
Lat/Lon coordinates for harbor entrance: N46°47.2'
                                           W90°50.8'

Port Superior Marina
34480 Port Superior Rd.
Bayfield WI 54814
715-779-5360
2 miles south of Bayfield on Highway 13
Monitors Channel 16
portsuperior.com
Transient slips available
Lat/Lon coordinates for harbor entrance: N46°47.2'
                                                  W90°50.8'

Port Wing Marina
9130 Beach Road
Port Wing, WI 54865
715-774-3555
portwingmarinaholidaypines.com
Transient slips available
Monitors Channel 16
Lat/Lon coordinates for harbor entrance: N46°47.6'
                                                  W91°23.2'

Roy's Point Marina
2 miles north of Bayfield
37735 Roy's Point Rd.
Bayfield, WI 54814
715-779-5025
royspoint.com
Transient slips available
Lat/Lon coordinates for harbor entrance: N46°50.5'
                                                  W90°47.0'

Schooner Bay Marina
3 ½ miles north of Bayfield
715-779-3266
Lat/Lon coordinates for harbor entrance: N46°52.9'
W90°46.1'

Siskiwit Bay Marina
Cornucopia, WI 54827
715-742-3337
Transient slips available
Lat/Lon coordinates for harbor entrance: N46°51.8'
W91°06.2'

Town of Bell Marina
Cornucopia, WI 54827
715-724-3363
Transient slips available
Lat/Lon coordinates for harbor entrance: N46°51.8'
W91°06.2'

Washburn Marina
715-373-5050
Transient slips available
Lat/Lon coordinates for harbor entrance: N46°40.0'
W90°53.1'

Lakeland Boating, *Lake Superior Ports O' Call*, Evanston: O'Meara-Brown Publications, Inc., 2001. This publication provides detailed information on several of the marinas in the Apostle Islands area. It can be ordered by phone (800-589-9491) or through their website (lakelandboating.com)

Museums
Ashland Historical Society Museum
509 W. Main Street
Ashland, WI 54806
715-682-4911
ashlandhistory.com

Bayfield Heritage Center
30 N. Broad Street
Bayfield, WI 54814
715-779-5958
bayfieldheritage.org

Bayfield Maritime Museum
131 S. 1st Street
Bayfield, WI 54814
715-779-9919
apostleisland.com/4.htm

Madeline Island Museum
226 Woods Ave.
LaPointe, WI 54850
715-747-2415
wisconsinhistory.org/madelineisland

Washburn Cultural Center
1 E. Bayfield Street (State Highway 13)
Washburn, WI 54891
715-373-5591

Mushrooms
Barron, George, *Mushrooms of Northeast North America*, Auburn: Lone Pine Publishing, 1999.

Lincoff, Gary H., *The Audubon Society Field Guide to North American Mushrooms*, New York: Alfred A Knopf, Inc., 1991.

National Park Service
Apostle Islands National Lakeshore Headquarters
415 Washington Ave
Bayfield, WI 54814
715-779-3397
nps.gov/apis
Summer hours-daily: 8:00 a. m. —6:00 p. m.
Non-summer hours-Mon-Fri: 8:00 a. m.—4:30 p. m.

Native American History
Warren, William, *History of the Ojibiway People*, St.
Paul: Minnesota Historical Society Press, 1984.

Armstrong, Benjamin, *Early Life Among the Indians*,
Press of A. W. Bowron, 1892. This out-of-print book
can be downloaded from Google. A historic account
by Benjamin Armstrong, who with Chief Buffalo and a
party of Ojibwe, traveled to Washington, D. C.,
enduring many hardships along the way, and
convinced President Millard Fillmore to rescind the
U. S. government order to remove the Ojibwe from
their historic homeland in the Apostle Islands area.

Northern Great Lakes Visitor Center
29270 County Road G
Ashland, WI 54806
715-685-9983
NGLVC.org
9:00AM-5:00PM daily
Located on County Road G, ½ mile west of junction
of US 2 and State Route 13, west of Ashland, WI

Plants/Trees
Bates, John, Illustrated by April Lehman, *Trailside
Botany*, Duluth: Pfeifer-Hamilton, 1995.

Judziewicz, Emmet J. and Koch, Rudy G., *Flora of the Apostle Islands*, Eastern National Park and Monument Association, 1995.

Phillips, Roger, *A Photographic Guide to More Than 500 Trees of North America*, New York: Random House, 1978.

Tekiela, Stan, *Trees of Wisconsin,* Cambridge, Minnesota: Adventure Publications, 2002.

Watts, May Theilgaard, *Tree Finder*, Rochester: Nature Study Guild Publishers, no date of publication.

Poison Ivy
See poison-ivy.com for good photos to aid in recognition

Recreational Reading Recommendations
Bishop, Hugh E, *The Night the Fitz Went Down*, Duluth: Lake Superior Port Cities, Inc., 2000. A chronology of the events relating to the sinking of the ore carrier, *Edmund Fitzgerald,* in a November 1975 Lake Superior "perfect storm".

Crowley, Peter, *Outdoor Follies*, Ashland: B & J Press, LLC, 2006. A compilation of humorous stories, some occurring in and around Chequamegon Bay.

Dennis, Jerry, *The Living Great Lakes*, New York: Thomas Dunne Books, 2003. The author's experiences traveling in the Great Lakes. Winner of "Best Book of 2003" award by the Outdoor Writers Association of America.

Keller, James M., *The Unholy Apostles*, Chelsea: Sheridan Books, 2004. Stories of the major shipwrecks occurring in the Apostle Islands.

Gilbertson, Jay, *Moon Over Madeline Island*, Kensington Publishing Corporation, 2005. Humorous novel of two older ladies moving to and starting up a home business on Madeline Island.

Newman, Lawrence, *Tales of a Nautical Novice: Lessons I Learned Boating In The Great Lakes*, Silver Millennium Publications, Inc., 2012 Compilation of stories describing the boating experiences of the author in the Great Lakes, in both sailboats and powerboats.

Lake Superior Magazine
325 Lake Ave South, 6th floor
Duluth, MN 55802
888-244-5253
218-722-5002

Sailboat Charters-Bareboat
Apostle Islands Yacht Charter Association
Madeline Island Yacht Club
800-821-3480
715-747-2983

Sailboats Inc.
100 Manypenny St.
Bayfield, WI 54814
800-826-7010 (reservations line)
715-779-3269
www.sailboats-inc.com

Superior Charters, Inc.
34475 Port Superior Rd
Bayfield, WI 54814
800-772-5124/715-779-5124
SuperiorCharters.com

Sailboat Charters-Captained
Animaashi Sailing Co.
888-272-4548
animaashi.com

Apostle Islands Yacht Charter Association
Madeline Island Yacht Club
800-821-3480/715-747-2983

Bayfield Charter Company
715-567-0112
bayfieldchartercompany.com

Catchun-Sun Charter
888-724-5494/715-779-3111
www.catchun-sunchartercompany.com

Dreamcatcher Sailing
800-682-1587/715-779-5561
wolfsongadventures.com/dreamcatcher/

Manitou Classic Sailing Charters
13 S. Second St. Unit #3
Bayfield, WI 54814
612-850-2981

Northern Breezes
Pike's Bay Marina
Bayfield, WI 54814
763-542-9707
NorthernBreezesSchool.com

Sailboats Inc
100 Manypenny St.
Bayfield, WI 54814
800-826-7010 (reservations line)
715-779-3269
www.sailboats-inc.com

Superior Charters, Inc.
34475 Port Superior Rd
Bayfield, WI 54814
800-772-5124/715-779-5124
SuperiorCharters.com

Viking Charters, LLP
Bayfield, WI 54814
507-236-4415
captaindave@vikingcharters.net

ZaBreeNa
84196 Pike's Bay Road
Bayfield, WI 54814
651-336-7357

Sailing Schools
Apostle Islands Yacht Charter Association
Madeline Island Yacht Club
800-821-3480/715-747-2983

Northern Breezes
763-542-9707
NorthernBreezesSchool.com

Sailboats Inc
100 Manypenny St.
Bayfield, WI 54814
800-826-7010/715-779-3269
www.sailboats-inc.com

144

Superior Charters, Inc.
34475 Port Superior Rd
Bayfield, WI 54814
800-772-5124
715-779-5124
SuperiorCharters.com

U. S. Coast Guard
Bayfield, WI
715-779-3950

Volunteers—Lighthouse Keepers and Park Interpreters
National Park Service
715-779-3397 Ext. 303
nps.gov/apis

Weather
National Weather Service
Marine Channels 1-10
nws.noaa.gov/om/marine/zone/gtlakes/ glctmz.htm
715-682-8822 Updated weather report (Long wait
normally experienced as full report cycles)

Ludlum, David M., *The Audubon Society Field Guide to
North American Weather*, New York: Alfred A. Knopf,
Inc., 1991.

Wildflowers
Tekiela, Stan, *Wildflowers of Wisconsin*, Cambridge:
Adventure Publications, Inc., 2000.

Peterson, Roger Tory, *Wildflowers-Peterson Field
Guide*, Boston: Houghton-Mifflin Co., 1996.

Wildlife

Daniel, Glenda and Sullivan, Jerry, *A Sierra Club Naturalist's Guide-The North Woods*, San Francisco: Sierra Club Books, 1981.

Stensaas, Mark, *Canoe Country Wildlife-A Field Guide to the North Woods and Boundary Waters*, Duluth: Pfeifer-Hamilton Publishers, 1993.

Sutton, Ann and Sutton, Myron, *The Audubon Society Nature Guide-Eastern Forests*, New York: Alfred A Knopf, Inc., 1992.

NON FOOD SUPPLIES
3-DAY SAILING TRIP

Sleeping bags
4 large garbage bags (13 gallon)-separate
  recyclables from trash
Paper Towels (2 rolls)
6 Zip Locs®-freezer type (3 qt/3 gal)
First aid kit (personal choice items) A kit is
  normally included in boat's standard supplies
French coffee press
Dish towel
Paper plates—non flimsy type
Aluminum foil for grill—heavy duty (3 feet)
GPS receiver with extra batteries
NOAA chart of Apostle Islands/calipers
Book on Apostle Islands describing nautical
  hazards/cruising guide
Toilet paper roll in Zip Loc®—may be plenty on
  boat but why take a chance. Biodegradable.
Personal flotation devices—inflatable waist
  type—wear at all times.
Binoculars
Camera
Propolene line(10 ft) for holding empty water
  jug over side of boat
Self-lighting charcoal (if needed—most boats
  have propane grills)
Soft duffels for personal items containing:
  Toilet kit
  Extra shirt/sweater
  Windbreaker

Dirty clothes bag
Rain gear
2 changes of underwear
3 pairs of thick cotton socks
Sweat suit or other nightwear—if desired
Hat for sun
Sunglasses
Moccasins—if desired
Flashlight
Bath towel-small
Washcloth and soap in Zip Loc®(if not in
  toilet kit)
Ditty bag containing:
  Vitamins, Rx, OTC medicines (ibuprofen,
    etc.)
  Eye glasses-compact—in hard case
  Waterproof matches/sunblock/insect
    repellent/chapstick

Notes: (1) Pickup 2 blocks of ice and 2 bags
             of ice chips on dock on morning of
             sailing.
        (2) If desired, pick up fish fillets at fish
             purveyors, south of Bayfield Marina, on
             morning of sailing.
        (3) Bareboat charters usually have
             pots, pans, cups, glasses,
             dishes, flatware, cooking utensils
             and cleaning supplies aboard.

SUGGESTED FOOD MENU
3-DAY SAILING TRIP

1ST Day: <u>Breakfast</u>: Egg Toss or other breakfast spot in Bayfield
<u>Lunch</u>: Ham and turkey sandwiches/ pickles/chips
<u>Dinner</u>: Spreadable and cut cheeses/ salsa/chips/crackers/white wine/precut salad with Italian dressing/lake trout fillets (grilled on aluminum foil) w/butter sauce and blanched almonds/grilled asparagus/ oatmeal raisin cookies

2nd Day: <u>Breakfast</u>: Breakfast cereal/blueberries /milk/coffee/boiled ham/ oranges /boiled eggs/rye bread/butter
<u>Lunch</u>: Ham and turkey sandwiches /pickles/chips
<u>Dinner</u>: Spreadable and cut cheeses/ summer sausage slices /crackers/red wine/precut salad with Italian dressing/New York strip steaks/ grilled Portobello mushrooms/grilled garlic bread/ oatmeal raisin cookies

3rd Day: <u>Breakfast</u>: Breakfast cereal /peach pieces in individual cups /milk/coffee/oranges/boiled eggs /rye bread/butter/boiled ham

149

<u>Lunch</u>: Ham and turkey
   sandwiches/Ramen soup
   /pickles/chips

<u>Extras (some optional)</u>:
Lettuce/tomatoes/mustard/mayo/salt and pepper
/apples /smoked meat sticks/large stick
pretzels/Old Bay fish seasoning/tartar sauce/steak
sauce/fine ground coffee /soft drinks/beer/3
gallons of water

<u>Notes</u>: (1) Place bread for sandwiches in hard
          container.
       (2) Coffee is prepared in French Press.
       (3) Cold milk should be placed in thermos
          bag for transfer to ice box.
       (4) Eggs can be hard boiled in advance.
       (5) Pack food items in labeled 2-gallon Zip
          Loc® bags (LUNCHES, 1ST DINNER,
          APPETIZERS, etc.)

THANKS AND ACKNOWLEDGMENTS

Ashland Daily Press and Ashland Weekly Press
(Predecessor to the Ashland Daily Press)

Burnham, Guy M, *The Lake Superior Country In History
And In Story*, Ashland: Paradigm Press, 1996

Federal Register of Committee Hearings on the
Establishment of the Apostle Islands National Lakeshore
(May and June 1967)

Jordahl, Howard "Bud", *A Unique Collection of Islands*,
Report on the Park Service website.

Leach, Thomas

Mackreth, Robert

Madeline Island Historical Museum-Exhibits

National Park Service personnel at the Apostle Islands
National Lakeshore Center—Jim Nepstad and Julie Van
Stappen

National Park Service publications

Neff, Marilyn (formerly Marilyn Allen)

Newman, Scott

Northern Great Lakes Visitor Center-Exhibits

Swartz, Carolyn

Thoreson, James

White, Theodore H., *The Making of a President—1960*, New
York: Atheneum Publishers, 1961.

A FEW PERSONAL NOTES

My personal attachment to the Apostle Islands arises from the fact that my father was born in Ashland in 1909 and remained in the area until the mid-1930's. As a young man he assisted his father, a naturalized immigrant from Finland, leading fishing parties into the far reaches of the Apostle Islands in search of lake trout. Although my father settled in the Chicago area after marrying my mother, our two-week summer vacations were spent in the Ashland area, when he returned home to visit his parents. Those annual two-week vacations for a kid from the closely packed neighborhood of Chicago's near-north side were like a taste of paradise.

Once, as a ten year old, I was a member of a family group that went on a deep lake fishing expedition. We left Ashland in mid-afternoon and motored out to Rocky Island, a five-hour trip in a covered motor launch with a twelve horsepower engine. After spending the night in the shelter of Rocky and South Twin islands we started out for Brownstone Island, now named North Twin, early the next morning, while it was still dark. We arrived off the west shore of Brownstone and began trolling just as the sky began to lighten. That area is now a fish refuge, closed to fishing. The lake trout we had that evening for dinner was one of the most memorable meals of my young life and made me a confirmed fish lover forever.

One of the enduring memories of that trip was the sensation of being in a boat on deep water. We had arrived in the shelter of Rocky Island shortly after a severe summer storm and the large waves from the lake had settled down into long deep swells—I would describe them as large rolling hills of water. Our boat was like a cork riding the crests of these swells and then settling into the valleys between them. On top you could see the islands and the open lake. At the bottom all you could see were walls of water. It was an experience I never forgot.

As the years passed I continued to come to the Ashland area and the Apostles, accompanied by my wife, Christine, a confirmed city girl, my three sons, Paul, Scott, Ron and their families. They have all come to appreciate the beauty of this area as much as I do. One of my granddaughters, Madeline, is named after the largest and most historic island in the Apostles. Chris's nephews, Scott and Wayne Hafenscher, have also been drawn to the beauty of the area. Today, from our summer home, located on a bluff overlooking Chequamegon Bay, east of Ashland, we look out over Long Island, Madeline Island, the north shore of the bay and the hills of the Bayfield Peninsula, always marveling at the changing panorama before us.

A few years before my dad passed away at age 90 I sat down with him and asked for his recollections of his experiences in the islands. Among the stories he told me was one I'd like to share.

One year, in the late 1920's, he and his dad stopped on Stockton Island early in the spring, near Quarry Bay. They were surprised to be greeted by a pack of emaciated dogs, which apparently had been left on the island to fend for themselves. The dogs were friendly and greeted them like long lost friends. Feeling sorry for them, my grandfather and dad set up a net on a nearby stream draining into the lake and in a short time had trapped hundreds of chubs, an oily bait fish, about eight inches long. They put these fish into a large metal barrel with some water and set a fire under it—all under the watchful eyes of the dogs. After the water was boiling furiously and the fish cooked, they pushed the barrel over on the sand. Even before the fish had thoroughly cooled, the dogs attacked their heaven-sent meal ravenously. They ate and ate and ate—until they simply couldn't eat any more. The dogs then just lay on the beach with bloated bellies. My dad said he and my grandfather had a good laugh and a sense of satisfaction as they watched those starving dogs satisfy their hunger.

The last visit my dad and I made to the Apostles was to Stockton Island where we walked the Julian Bay Trail together. He was in his late 80's at the time and when we reached the scenic bog overlook near the end of the trail he sat down on a recently cut large tree stump to rest. I never pass that spot, now overgrown with small pine trees, without remembering him sitting there, looking out over that vista.

He loved the islands and passed that gift on to me.

AND FINALLY—A COUPLE OF POEMS INSPIRED BY MY TIME IN THE ISLANDS

Beach Stones

Hold them in your hand,

Tightly.

They will speak to you,

Of their creation,

In fiery throes,

Long ago.

Of their passage through time,

Of their movement by glaciers,

To this beach,

Where you now stand.

To hear of this journey,

Hold them in your hand,

Tightly.

The Paths We Tread

How many have gone before me,

Down this trodden path,

Through these dark woods?

 I see their faces,

Going back in time,

One fading into another,

To the earliest people who dwelled here.

We are one in this experience,

Moving down this path,

Of past and present.

I am one of a timeless band,

An unbroken chain of souls,

Experiencing these woods,

Hearing its sounds,

At one with nature,

With those who went before.

awrence Newman is the President of Silver Millennium ublications, Inc. and author of numerous books, including three about his favorite subject—the Apostle Islands, an archipelago of twenty two islands located off Wisconsin's northern shore in western Lake Superior, home of the Apostle Islands National Lakeshore, deemed the most pristine national park in the United States. He has also written books on other subjects, including self-publishing, boating and quote compilations. In his prior life he was a Senior Vice President and Chief Financial Officer for Underwriters Laboratories, Inc. before he retired in 2001, after eighteen years with that company.

anyone interested in pursuing the publication of his or her own book is welcome to contact him at silvermillpub@gmail.com. Books published by Silver Millennium Publications, Inc. can be viewed at silvermillpub.com, Amazon.com, and Barnesand-noble.com. Retailer's inquiries are also welcome.

NOTES

NOTES